S0-ACC-897

If the Woodsman is Late

is Late

Tales of growing up in a society that respected personal ownership of firearms

Copyright © 2011 Mathew Paust

ISBN 978-1-61434-499-5

All rights reserved. No part of this publication may be reproduced, stored in a retrieval system, or transmitted in any form or by any means, electronic, mechanical, recording or otherwise, without the prior written permission of the author.

Published in the United States by Booklocker.com, Inc., Bangor, Maine.

Many of the stories in If the Woodsman is Late are personal histories. The author has changed many of the names of people in these stories, and in some cases he changed other identifying characteristics. The following names are pseudonyms: Mark, Bubba, Laurie, Steve, Butch, Roger, Cal, Terri, Miss Fortune, Achal, Rami, Klaus, Pete, Kenny, and Elmer Fudd.

All names, characters, places and incidents in the fiction stories are products of the author's imagination or are used fictitiously. Any resemblance to actual people is unintentional and coincidental.

All images reproduced in this book are either the sole property of the author or are licensed for use here by iStockphoto or Howard Schechtman. Mr. Schechtman designed the book's front and back covers. His original image of a scene from Flannery O'Connor's short story A Good Man is Hard to Find appears with a story inside the book and on the back cover. More of Mr. Schechtman's art can be found on his Web site at www.howi3.deviantart.com

Any people depicted in stock imagery provided by iStockphoto are models, and such images were used for illustrative purposes only.

Printed in the United States of America on acid-free paper.

Bartleby Scriveners Assoc.
2011

If the Woodsman is Late

Tales of growing up in a society that respected personal ownership of firearms

Mathew Paust

Dedicated to the memory of some good folks: Joe Zambone, Lou Alessi, Jim Vollink, Cal and Mark

ACKNOWLEDGMENTS

I owe a deep debt of gratitude to my wife, Angela, our daughter, Sarah and our two sons, Michael and Joshua for their love and understanding during the reclusive hours, days, weeks, months and, yes, years I, as have most writers, devoted to the unavoidable solitude, both physical and emotional, which is vital in luring the ideas and then the words out of their hiding places in the mind's secluded archives. Your steadfast loyalty and trust that what I've been doing all this time was worthy have kept me feeling as secure as any writer can hope for in a time when, with a few joyous exceptions, reading for pleasure in our culture appears to be going the way of the dinosaur, the passenger pigeon and cursive writing.

I would also like to thank, without using the bottom-of-my-heart cliché, if possible, Doc Hudson, for his kind advice, and my friends and fellow writers in the blogging community Open Salon – with an extra nod to the Rules Committee – for their encouragement, their advice, warm friendship and, what the hell, their fiscal support of my efforts by buying my first book, *Executive Pink*, and pimping it to others in the world at large. The three who stuck their necks out furthest for me, i.e. by name, are Sharon Watts, Alisa Spitzberg and Richard Brown. You guys, in my book, are the cat's pajamas and I thank you from the bottom of my heart...oops.

Table of Contents

Forward

Despite impressions you might have taken from the title and cover of this book that it is devoted solely to guns, please know that while guns do play a role in most of the stories, many are completely gun free. If you like the way I tell stories but don't like guns there's plenty for you here. In truth, guns have played a significant role in my life from as far back as I remember. In today's world this would be unusual. Today a boy can be expelled from school for drawing a picture of a gun. When I was a boy my best friend brought a real gun to school for show and tell. While an adult eyebrow or two might have been raised, no one called the police. He carried the German Luger openly from home several blocks away, dazzled his classmates with his uncle's war trophy, and carried it home again.

It is this contrast between yesterday and today that interests me, and I hope will interest you, as well. Although my biases may be obvious, I will do my best not to batter you with them. One of the first rules of good writing is not to tell but to show. I have attempted to follow that rule in these stories. I don't consider it my job to try to change your mind on anything, but I can't deny I'd be delighted if my stories helped you to see and understand a point of view that might be different from one you already hold.

I've included the gun-free stories to help you gain a more rounded perspective of a man who otherwise might be seen only in the glaring light of what has become a highly adversarial issue. To those at one extreme of this spectrum, who might see someone like me as a stereotypical gun nut, unstable and dangerous, I hope to reveal a gentle, good-humored family man who shares most of the same fundamental values as they. Folks at the spectrum's other extreme might find me lacking sufficient militant fiber to carry the Second Amendment battle flag into the enemy camp, at any cost. They may be right. I don't know.

Carl von Clausewitz defined war as "the extension of politics by other means." From this view, the politics of gun ownership is still in play. At stake are hearts and minds. To this and to life I write.

I've arranged these stories in no particular order, although I have grouped several of them by subject. The newspaper stories are together, if not in any particular sequence, as are those reminiscences of my Army days. I've dropped in a whimsical piece here and there for variety. The fiction should be readily identifiable, but to avoid any confusion I've indicated in the table of contents those that came entirely from my imagination.

Flashback
(fiction)

It was chilly when she awoke only minutes from sunrise. Damn, she thought, shivering under the flannel sheet and comforter in her dark bedroom and remembering it had started snowing when she'd turned in last night. Seeing the dusty flakes swirling across the deck outside her kitchen, she had felt the childlike delight that always accompanied her first glimpse of a new snow, when, regardless of whether there was anyone to hear her she always uttered with a trace of wonderment, "It's snowing!" Last night the innocent charm of these words dissipated almost instantly, pushed aside by the irritated thought that what the hell was it doing snowing halfway through April?

She pulled the covers around her, assuming the alarm hadn't gone off yet. Ten more minutes, what the hell. When she next awoke the mysteries of darkness had been replaced by the flat indifferent light of another day. "Shit," she said aloud after squinting at her digital clock and realizing she'd forgotten to set the alarm. It was nearly 6:30. She had a half hour to do her morning preps and be on her way to work. Gotta skip breakfast this morning, she groused silently, hurling the covers off and pivoting out of bed. A momentary shock awakened her further when she looked out the window facing her backyard and saw a smooth white landscape stretching back to a dark green row of frosted Norway pines. Whew. Beautiful, but no thank you. At least it had stopped snowing, she thought.

She scrapped her intention to wash her hair this morning, knowing the drive would take longer than usual. Holding her head away from the water, she showered quickly. She had dressed, cleared a spot for Torquy's bowl on the deck and filled it with Purina Cat Chow and was backing her SUV out of her driveway by 6:55. Her tires crunching through the four-inch layer of snow, it was slow going down the private, gravel road that served the four other homes in her neighborhood, and she was glad to see when she reached the highway there'd been enough morning traffic already to have tamped the snow down fairly well. She reached for the hand mic on the console under the dash, pulled it up to her mouth and squeezed the talk button.

"Unit Two ten-eight," she said, her voice crisply neutral. The radio crackled awake and a female voice rode in on the static, "That's a ten-four, Unit Two. Good morning, Major."

"Morning, Stella. How're the roads?"

"Working two ten-fifties. No pee-eyes. Repeat, that's negative pee-eyes."

"Ten-four, Stella. I'll be ten-twenty-six in fifteen." She had decided to skip Hardee's for coffee. There'd be plenty at work, and donuts and Danish. She was trying to eat healthier, but... She sighed as she replaced the hand mic in its holder, feeling glad at least the snow had stopped. Most accidents occurred when snow was falling. Heavy snowfall, especially if it was blowing, obscured and distorted vision She kept a lookout for motorists in trouble. There would be at least one vehicle in the ditch on a morning like this. Not this morning, though, it pleased her to find. So far so good. She pulled into the parking area behind the station. Oddly, the Chief's SUV was in its spot blanketed with snow, with no tracks to indicate it had been driven since last night. A city plow had scraped the rest of area, so she parked in her designated spot next to the Chief's.

The sharp bark of a crow cut through the crunch of her shoes as she walked to the rear door of the two-story brick building. Looking up she spotted the raucous black bird balancing on one of the two floodlights affixed to the masonry above the door. The bird dipped its head as if to acknowledge her, then, with a sudden lunge and a series of throaty calls it leaped off its perch and rose over the parking lot. The sporadic bursts of caws and frantic beat of its wings as it struggled to maintain altitude in the cold dead air vaguely offended her, as if the bird had judged her and now was fleeing her presence.

She used a card-key to unlock the door, then entered and climbed the nearby cement stairs to the second floor. She walked down a hallway past several offices and the investigators' bay. All of the doors were closed, indicating either nobody was in yet or they weren't ready for visitors. Official starting time for the day shift and administrators was 8, half an hour away. She walked past her own office and the Chief's secretary's to the end of the hall and tapped lightly on the frosted window of the Chief's door.

"Harry?" she called softly.

"Yeah? Agnes? That you?" It was the Chief's raspy voice, shaking off sleep it seemed and...there was something else. She turned the knob and pulled the door open a crack.

"Morning, Chief." Whatever it was she'd heard in his voice persuaded her to drop the informality.

"Come in. Sit down." He wasn't smiling when she stepped into the spartan office, which contained only a wooden desk with a couple of wooden chairs on a threadbare carpet in front of it. A filing cabinet with four drawers abutted one wall opposite a bookcase against the other. The bookcase held stacks of law enforcement related magazines and what appeared to be several law books. Holding her boss's cool gaze Agnes lowered herself almost cautiously into one of chairs. "Something wrong, Chief?" she ventured.

He stared at her a moment longer through reading glasses that lent a professorial air to his wide, jowly face. It appeared she'd interrupted him doing paperwork, but she noticed the camping cot in a corner behind him he usually kept folded up. It was unfolded now and contained a pillow and blanket. He broke off his gaze and nodded toward the cot.

"Trying to catch up on some paperwork," he grumbled. "I get more work done at night without all the busy bees buzzing around." His thick fingers scraped over whiskery stubble that covered the lower half of his face. He tried to smile. "Just getting ready to shave when you knocked."

He stood, and Agnes saw that his normally crisp white shirt and pressed blue uniform trousers were rumpled. He wasn't a tall man, and his thick chest and neck always reminded her of pictures she'd seen of a barrel cactus. The bristles of what remained of his steel-gray hair added to this impression. He turned and fussed at a small table behind his desk, and then brought her a cup of steaming coffee and a paper plate containing a couple of pastries he said were left over from yesterday. Seated back at his desk, with his own coffee and pastries, he got down to business.

"I wish you had been there yesterday, Agnes," he said, his voice softer than before.

"Chief, it was your day. You deserved it. And my mother really did need me. She's gotten another infection."

"Sorry to hear that. I hope she's better. But yesterday was more yours than mine or anybody's. If you hadn't put those butts in the freezer we'd have no case. We'd have no suspect."

"I was just doing my job, Harry. You'd have done the same."

He reached up and removed his glasses, revealing eyes with irises so black that by themselves they gave him a fierceness that inspired his Richmond colleagues to call him Darth Vader. Resting his chin in a vee formed by his joined fists, he leaned forward now and fixed his black lasers on the woman before him.

"No, ma'am, I would not," he growled. "In all my years with RPD homicide the only thing we ever did with cigarette butts was check them for brand. We didn't know what DNA was. We didn't really know what it was ten years ago at the laundry. But you put them in the freezer. Without those butts those murders would have never been solved."

"You got the confessions."

"I got 150 confessions. People like to confess. Feeble minded people. Nuts. They come out of the woodwork in a case like this. Without those cigarette butts, my confessions aren't worth the paper they're typed on. It was you, Agnes. I hired you right out of college, and you took what you learned, and what I laughed at – and I apologize now for that – and followed the book, your book. The college book. I know you didn't know how it would turn out. Nobody could know then what we know now about DNA, so maybe it is all just luck. But, hey, fifty percent of police work is just luck. I just wish you had been there yesterday."

"Harry, I had a terrible feeling this morning when I drove in here and saw your car covered with snow.

The Chief put his glasses back on and leaned back in his swivel chair, his eyes fixed on Agnes but with a different face, a look of puzzlement with a pall of sadness over his features. He said nothing, but stared awhile longer, then slowly nodded. He'd taken a deep breath when she said this, and now let it out in a sigh that told her more than any words. Tears glistened in the corners of her eyes.

"I haven't looked outside yet," he said. "It was snowing last night when I decided to stay here. I was hoping it wouldn't be much.

She blurted, "It's the snow. I remember the snow more than anything else, more than finding the bodies back by the boiler room, which was the most awful thing I had ever seen. I still dream about them. But it's the snow I remember first. It's the snow and the cars I see in my mind. Their cars parked out back, covered with snow and no tracks, so we knew they hadn't gone home, that they were still in there. We knew, I knew, they were all dead before we even went inside."

The Chief stood again and came around his desk. He walked behind her and put a hand on her shoulder. "Agnes, you probably won't believe me when I say this, but the snow is what bothers me most about this, too. It's bothered me every time I see snow on the ground and every time I think about this case. I handled thousands of killings in Richmond. Thousands. Many of them so brutal and terrible I don't know how I ever get any sleep at night. But you wanna know something? This was the worst goddam one of all.

"And I'm not sure why. Maybe I was getting too old, too burned out, you know? I came here after Erma died and I didn't want to work in the city anymore and deal with the depravity and the endless inhumanity...oh, Agnes, I thought I was so damned tough and professional. And I was. I was pretty damned good, but it eats at you. Eats and eats at you. Eats away your soul. And I came here thinking this would be a piece of cake. A small town, friendly folks, hardly any crime, and then this. I knew those people. Most of them. Been to their homes as a guest. They never had a chance, kneeling on the floor so long their knees were bruised. And then...shot..." He paused to choke back waves of memory. "Shot..." his voice broke, but he forced the words out between sobs, "...shot like goddam dogs on the floor, kneeling on the goddam floor. They weren't drug dealers or pimps or lowlifes. They were decent..."

His sobs won out. Agnes turned in her chair and placed her hand over the one on her shoulder.

We Were Cowboys Then

Guns and I go back to life before kindergarten. I assume this because of the gun incident in my morning kindergarten class, which is my earliest particular gun memory. There must have been precedents, as I remember that the gun in the kindergarten incident, while fascinating, was not an alien object. It was made of some cheap cast alloy. A cap gun, I imagine. Steve, the new guy, used it to bop Butch, the bully, on the head, making him cry. This was a sea change moment in our class of about 30 five-year-olds.

The year was 1946. World War II – the last of the "good" wars – had ended less than a year before. Guns had helped us beat the Heinies and the Japs. Guns were good. Kids were not at risk of being expelled from school for drawing pictures of guns or, hard as it is to believe, of being charged with a crime for bringing a real gun to school for show and tell. This actually happened several years later when I met the boy who would become my best friend carrying a German Luger in plain sight as he headed home after dazzling his classmates with his uncle's war trophy.

"I will deaded you," he announced, pointing the black military sidearm at me as we approached each other in the front stairwell, me staring in wonderment. Mark, was his name. He was a new student, whom I'd seen but never spoken with until now. We quickly learned we were neighbors and walked home together, Mark holding the pistol in his hands for all the world to see.

This was a time when certainties were established early and went unquestioned, at least through a boy's eyes. Good was good, bad was bad and gray was for old people's hair. The kindergarten incident played out with no mitigating ambiguities. From the moment Steve bopped and Butch cried the two became archetypes straight from our cowboy-movie-fueled boys' culture. Steve – tall, slim, blonde, taciturn, modest, the Randolph Scott sheriff; Butch – big, black-haired and blustery, the classic villain. They remained thus for the next several years until Steve and his family moved away. They remain thus in my mind even today, more than half a century later, despite my path crossing briefly with each of theirs under incongruous circumstances as young adults.

The unpretentious little club with the pretentious name "Metropolitan" sat off the highway in a ragged commercial strip near a college town. It was still a hangout mostly for university students. Its main attraction, besides no cover charge, was surprisingly good live music. Whoever booked the acts was able to snag name performers such as Conway Twitty, who was on stage my last night out before reporting to be sworn in and bused to basic training as an Army private.

It was mid-September 1963. Kennedy was well into his third year as president and U.S. troops were two years shy of removing their "advisory" gloves in Vietnam. I was joining the Army because I'd flunked out of school and lost my draft deferment. Enlisting, I figured, would give me choices other than infantry. The trade-off meant I'd be in uniform four years instead of two.

A couple of friends were taking me to "Metro's" for a farewell beer. The combo's pounding melodic bass welcomed us into the club as the dominant sound over a background buzz of conviviality, the laughter and chatter, the chair scrapes and clinks and clunks of glassware on wooden tables. Inside, the familiar bar smell engulfed our olfactory senses, heavy with tobacco smoke and fermented brews, with an occasional tease of feminine cosmetics.

The dominant personage in the room was Twitty. A big man with big hair, he towered on the narrow stage against the back wall. Propitious, it struck me, that Twitty was belting out the chorus of Lee and Goodman's *Let the Good Times Roll*. It was early enough to find a few unoccupied tables. We picked one a row back from a dance floor so cramped the two or three couples bobbing and trying to gyrate on it were hard pressed to keep from bumping each other.

I was finishing my second draft beer when the band took a break. Twitty unstrapped his guitar and set it down and sat himself down on a folding chair near the back of the stage. In the moments before recorded music replaced the live I overheard a snippet of conversation between two young women at a table at the edge of the dance space directly in front of the stage. "He asked me to meet him afterwards," said one, tilting her head at the stage, her voice arched as if saying "ewwww." Her companion vocalized the implied disgust. They were loud enough to ensure anyone nearby could hear them, Twitty included, but he never looked up. It might have been unintended coincidence but his first song after the break was from his newly released album. It was his cover of *Fever*.

By then I'd had my last reunion with Butch. I hadn't seen him in about ten years and didn't recognize him at first. My friends had wandered off during the break and I was alone at the table when a waiter brought me a fresh, unordered beer. "Compliments of the guy at the bar," he said, nodding at a hulking figure on a stool at the horseshoe bar next to the kitchen entrance. "Whoops," thought I. The man turned then just enough so our eyes met. I had no choice but to get up and walk over.

"Hey, remember me?" he said in a deep unfamiliar voice. "Yeah. You look familiar," I lied. "Butch," he said, and the years fell away as if they'd never been. It was Butch's wolfishly merry grin that took me back. I'd last seen him wielding a wooden bench in the locker room after gym class, the mean-spirited teacher staving off the bench with both hands. The rest of us cleared out. Butch never returned to school. We'd become friendly over the years up to then. He and his dad lived in a trailer on my paper route and I always looked forward to seeing him outside and would stop to chat.

He'd just been released from prison, where he served several years for receiving stolen property, he said. I sat at the bar with him, finished my beer and bought us another round. He teared up when I told him I was off to the Army. "I'd give anything to go with you," he said, explaining that the Army wouldn't take him with his record. My memory of Butch closes there, with us sitting at the bar, his black hair unruly, bushy mustache adorning his big square face, tears filling his eyes.

I didn't see Steve again from the day he moved away in elementary school until my first day of classes at the university after returning from my Army tour in Germany. I was meandering around the sprawling campus re-familiarizing myself with its geography when I paused at a construction site near on old departmental building. Someone was working in an excavation with a shovel. What struck me was the large brown mole at the base of his hairline. I'd never seen anyone else with such a mark. The hair was short and nearly white, just as I remembered it.

"Steve?" I called into the pit. The worker straightened up, turned and I knew it was him. He looked almost the same. Rail thin, handsome, chiseled features, light blue eyes. Randolph Scott. "It's Mattie," I said. The shy smile of his childhood stretched his face just enough to acknowledge recognition. We spoke briefly. He was embarrassed, and, then, so was I. There really wasn't much to say. We made no plans to meet for a drink. "See you around," I said. He nodded, waved a hand and went back to his shovel. I never saw him again.

Nightmare on Maple Street

The last time I saw Roger was at our 15th high school class reunion. I've skipped most of them since, including our 50th last fall. But it was good to see Roger. We'd been neighbors and friends. We laughed at the same sorts of things. Irreverent.

He'd quit a good job on the West Coast and was making a good living, he said, playing the horses at several tracks up and down the coast. We talked a good bit at the reunion. The years fell away. We got a little drunk. One subject that never came up was the Bubba thing. No need to talk about that. No need to remember.

The last time I saw Bubba was several years later when I was home visiting family. He was the attendant at the gas station where I stopped to fill up. If he recognized me he didn't let on. I didn't let on, either.

The Bubba thing had happened in an earlier life. Roger and I were ten or eleven (good god, I hope we weren't older than that) and Bubba was five or six years older. He was a lot bigger physically than either of us. I don't believe he went to school. He rarely spoke and always looked dour and mean. His half-sister, Laurie, was four or five, too young for my sister and her friends, who were seven or eight, but who had no friends her own age so was always hanging around. She and Bubba lived with their mother around the corner on our block.

Laurie was a pest.

One fall afternoon when I was raking leaves for a bonfire we'd planned for that evening next to our driveway, Roger walked over from his house kitty corner from us. We got to talking and I took a break. Then up rode Laurie on her tricycle.

"Hi, Mafyew. Hi," she said sweetly. We ignored her. She persisted. Suddenly Roger, ever prone to act on reckless impulse, picked up the iron rake and waved it over Laurie's head.

"Go home!" he shouted. Terrified, the little girl wheeled around and began pedaling down the sidewalk. This awakened Roger's hound instincts and he chased after her. Then my spaniel instincts kicked in and I followed. With Roger waving the rake we chased the frantically pedaling Laurie the entire length of our block on Maple Street and around the corner until Laurie hopped off her trike and, sobbing, scurried into her house.

Almost instantly the front door swung open and out burst Bubba. The race was on. Roger's hound instincts, sharper by a tad than my spaniel's, took the lead and he was around the corner before I got off the mark. But I wasn't far behind. I didn't dare look back to see how close Bubba was, but I could hear his huffing and the thumps of his sneakers on the sidewalk. I focused on trying to catch up with Roger and blocked out any defeatist thoughts the monster behind might be gaining on me.
I read a lot of comic books in those days, and the phrase "Feets don't fail me now" popped out of the archive in my head. I had never before and have never since - even when running track or

playing football - run so goddamned fast. Had I been older I might easily have herniated or torn a groin muscle.

Bubba's effort likely came nowhere near the heartfelt passion impelling Roger and me from the jaws of certain annihilation, as he was still huffing and thumping at least half a house away when we made it to mine and dashed inside quicker than Laurie had hers moments earlier.

We heard him thump up our porch steps as I slammed the door shut, and now Bubba was shouting. I've blocked the words out of my memory, as I imagine Roger has also, although I doubt Bubba's vocabulary included quite as many of the humiliating variations I was to learn years later from Army drill sergeants.

My spaniel's id took over at this point and I led Roger to the upright piano almost against the wall at a right angle from the front door. There was just enough room for us to squeeze behind the lovely instrument, where we cowered and listened to Bubba cursing and trying to knock our door down with his Goliath fists.

Time is compressed in my memory now. I can't tell you how long the cowering, cursing and pounding went on, but I do recall with vivid clarity the cavalry's appearance in the body of my dad, arriving home from work to find Boo Radley raising hell on his front porch. My dad sent Bubba home, but not before learning something mysteriously untoward had occurred involving Bubba and me.

Still behind the piano, I asked him if it was safe for us to come out. He undoubtedly struggled to keep a straight face as we explained the situation. Afterward, my dad sent Roger home, then escorted me down the street and around the corner to the house of horror, where I mumbled some apologetic tripe to a still-sobbing Laurie, now in her mother's comforting arms as a dour Bubba loomed nearby.

I don't remember what happened to the rake.

Scent of a Gun

There was magic in the doorway between my mother's kitchen and the adjacent room, our dining room. The first floor of our side of the rented house consisted of a row of rooms starting with "the back room," then the kitchen, dining room, living room and finally a screened porch accessible through tall windows that slid up and down. Both kitchen and living room could be entered from outside. The kitchen's we called "the back door" while the living room's was the front. Our dining room, caught in the middle, had no such portals to the world at large, but it had other doors – one leading to the cellar and the other, at right angles, to the second floor where our bedrooms and the only bathroom in our side of the house were located.

I was toddling from the kitchen to the dining room with a freshly baked gingerbread man that my mother had decorated just like the one in the story, the story that had the unhappy ending where the fox gives the smartass cookie a ride across the river on his nose and then snaps him up never to be seen again. I cried a river when my mother read me that story at bedtime. So next day she changed the ending for me by baking a real gingerbread man. "It's ready, Mathew," her musical voice called from the kitchen. I had been waiting impatiently in the dining room for her to finish decorating it just like the one in the story, except that she substituted raisins for the fictional currants used for the eyes, nose, smiling mouth and buttons down the front.

Nearly delirious with anticipation, yet skeptical that my mother had really rescued The Gingerbread Man from the fox's stomach, I tentatively entered the kitchen. Good gawd amighty THERE HE WAS, smiling at me as if about to hop off the table and flee, crying gleefully, "Run, run as fast as you can. You can't catch me, I'm the gingerbread man!" Still warm from the oven, the light brown anthropomorphic fellow, about as big as Bobby, my favorite teddy bear, smelled good, too. I began to experience fox-like gastric impulses, which intruded rudely into my little fantasy of saving the fabled victim from...I'm really not sure, now that I think of it, as there were no foxes in the immediate vicinity to my knowledge. So it was with a mixture of fantastic fulfillment, vague gastric interest and the sheer joy of possession that I lifted my gingerbread man off the waxed paper and, holding him carefully – my mother warned me several times to "be careful, hold him carefully" – with both hands, made it to the magic door with the intention of re-entering the dining room where my father waited to help me celebrate the miracle.

Never happened. Tripped on the damned door sill and baby go boomp, crumbling cookie into enough pieces baby do naught but sit on floor and cry his shattered little heart out. During much motherly consolation, interrupted by spasms of paternal laughter, the gingerbread man was repaired, somewhat, but it had lost the lifelike gleam in its mischievous eye, and I'm quite certain there was encouragement to freely indulge my vulpine urges, which I did and have been unable to resist the aroma and taste of gingerbread ever after.

The redolence of burnt gunpowder has a bio-psychic effect on me as well, pricking into the id and arousing limbic energies. A whiff of gun smoke triggers memory packets that reach back to my earliest outdoor adventures as a boy. The genesis of this olfactory temporal link is back-lit by the same magical kitchen doorway several years forward from the cookie tragedy. I sat in the same chair at the dining room table where I had waited for my mother to retrieve the gingerbread man from the fox's belly.

This time I watched my father step over the treacherous threshold into the kitchen, carrying a small metal toy pistol. The toy was designed to fire tiny caps of gunpowder on a paper roll that fed through the breech. Pulling the trigger activated levers inside the gun that rocked the hammer back and advanced the caps up through a slot at the rear of the gun. Coordination of these functions was such that as each cap moved under the hammer the controlling levers ended their cycle, releasing the hammer to slam down on the cap igniting the gunpowder with a *bang* and a puff of smoke.

 My father had given me the toy gun, but not the caps. They were dangerous, he said. I wasn't old enough. The disappointment in my entire being at coming so close to my dream of having a gun that went bang must have touched my father to the extent that he took the little pistol into the kitchen. "Wait here," he said, his smile and a note of promise in his voice playing nicely to my hopes of a happy ending.

My wait this time was less anxious, a tad perplexed, as I strained to hear whatever sounds might emanate from the kitchen. There were occasional soft murmurs as my father and mother conferred, I presume. Nothing metallic, nothing tympanic, nothing, except the occasional murmurs, which heightened my bewilderment, my curiosity and, thus, my impatience. When the murmurs ceased and my father did not return to the dining room I guessed he'd gone into "the back room," an unheated storage area off the kitchen. This room served as a receptacle for the kinds of things and odors ordinarily found in attics. It was a fascinating, mysterious room where a boy could spend hours indulging his imagination while poking among the family memorabilia. This I did, often.

Sniffing carefully for any change in the balance of smells there, I checked the room soon after my father brought the gun back to me, his eyes reflecting my eager expectancy as he placed it into my hands. I knew instantly what I now had. A gun with a real gun smell. The smell of a gun that had just been fired. A wild, acrid exotic smell, the likes of which I'd never tasted previously yet somehow knew to be authentic. My father took the secret of what he'd done to the grave. He'd performed an act of pure magic, and magicians never reveal. I understood this then. Perhaps a roll of caps had come with the gun, and he'd simply put them aside. There'd been no bang, so, if indeed it had been a cap, he could simply have torn one open, poured the powder onto a saucer and ignited it with a match. Perhaps it was just a match that gave my gun its new, thrilling and indelible flavor. I thought of this then, and ruled it out – maybe because I needed to believe it was something less mundane.

First Gun

The stump is vivid in my memory. If I were to sculpt a model of it in the bathtub, as Richard Dreyfuss did with his Devil's Tower obsession in Close Encounters, I could probably come pretty close. It was my mecca as a youngster with his first rifle, a Mossberg bolt action .22 carbine with a sort of Mannlicher stock that had a hinged forearm that I could pull down to give it a tommygun look.

I can still smell the grownup blend of odors the carbine gave off. These were the combined smells that filled the inside of the seed and feed store where my dad bought the carbine as an Easter present for me. I was probably about 10 or 11. I often visited the store with my dad, as it was across the street from his law office and he knew the proprietor. I spotted the carbine in a small rack behind the counter along with several other long guns, and, after the first time I picked it up and swung down the forearm, I was hooked. Instant lust.

I was too old and savvy to make a big deal out of my new romance at that time, but I'm pretty sure I conveyed my serious interest in the carbine to my dad along with a serious-yet-low-key hint that when I became old enough to own a gun, this was the one I would like. If it didn't shake out quite like this,  then for sure my dad, who was fairly savvy himself, would have picked up on the special relationship growing between me and the carbine as I examined it with exceeding care again and again and again, each time we visited the store.

Yet, when Easter rolled around, my sophistication melted into giddy surprise when it became clear that the carbine was now mine.

That very day was my first visit to the stump.

The stump - huge, the remains of a very mature oak - was located beside the runway of a small airfield that stretched between a cow pasture and a U.S. highway. It was where my father had learned to fly and where he kept a succession of small airplanes, including a Piper Cub, a Taylorcraft and one or two Cessnas. I usually accompanied him when he visited the place, either to check on the plane, work on it, fiddle with it or sometimes even to take it up. I had many a ride in the days before I discovered the stump.

This is where we went that Easter Sunday and where we tried out the carbine, shooting at a few tin cans we'd brought with us. The stump became my "range" over the next several years. It was where I learned marksmanship and gun handling skills, and where I bonded as a shooter with Mark - friend, neighbor and eventual business partner, who had a plastic-stocked Remington Model 66, which I liked, a lot, but wouldn't have dreamed of trading my carbine for. Such a preposterous exchange was never broached between us.

Death in the Tall Grass

It struck without warning. No thunderclap, not even a rolling rumble. Just cr*ack*. The jolt shot across and up with a shriek from the right side of my face deep into the cerebral cortex, leaving me frightened and undone. It was what my dentist dismissively called "an electric shock," which happened whenever a spoon or fork made contact with one of my silver molar fillings. This zap happened with nothing in my mouth but stewed meat. I stopped chewing and looked at my mother.

"What's the matter, Mathew?" she said, lines of concern crinkling the upper third of her warm round face.

I was afraid to speak. Afraid to move my jaw. I simply looked at her, my face undoubtedly crinkled even more than hers, and slowly, cautiously worked my tongue back to the molar area. That's where it was, a tiny ball of lead, about the size of a peppercorn. I've no doubt the relief from this discovery spread over my face in a wave that induced my mother to relax her face, thus allowing my father, who sat opposite her at the kitchen table and had been tuning his antennae to signals of something possibly amiss, to stand down as well.

I worked the pellet forward and spit it out, sending it hurtling onto my plate with a surprisingly distinct *plink*.

"Shot, huh?" My father wasn't much of a hunter, but he'd bought me the shotgun and knew enough to quickly solve the mystery of the mini-crisis. My mother at first wondered if maybe it was a bone chip, which it easily might have been. Having grown up on a farm, she had helped me gut the rabbit and skin it. She'd found several of the lead pellets cutting it up for the stew pot and was disappointed she hadn't gotten them all.

Neither parent was enthusiastic about the meat but they ate enough to be good sports. It was tough and stringy. I chewed dutifully and swallowed most of what was on my plate before acknowledging defeat. It was awful, but I'd killed it and was trying to live up to the code of the hunter as represented by my favorite columnists in *Field & Stream*, one of them a distant relative who wrote as Gil Paust. In those articles rabbit was described as a delicacy, tender and delicious. I mentioned this.

"Well," my mother said earnestly, "he was probably an older rabbit. Their meat would be tougher." The thought had never entered my considerations, neither the gender nor the age. My considerations were becoming complicated.

"How old do you think he was?" This was me, suddenly more discombobulated than I'd been after the tooth shock. I could still sing the words to *Peter Cottontail* and had been enthralled by Uncle Wiggly stories not many years prior as my mother would read an episode each night at bedtime. I was a big Bugs Bunny fan. Anthropomorphism was rearing its unwelcome head at the dinner table.

"They can live a long time," my dad contributed, his cruel streak awakening as

25

he sensed where my head was headed. He added, "He was probably an old grandpa."

This came with the disabling force of a blow to the solar plexus. I struggled gamely to eat the rest of the meat on my plate, spitting out another pellet or two before finally concluding my rite of passage, fighting tears.

Old grandpa was the first mammal I had killed. To this day I can hear him screaming, out of sight in the grass where he'd run after I blasted him with the 20-gauge bird shot. I stalked in after him and found him lying on his side, writhing and shrieking in agony. I shot at him again at nearly point blank range. I assumed I had missed because the screaming didn't stop. It took a third shot to end what had started as something I'd dreamed of for years now become ghastly. But I manned up, took him home, cleaned his pellet-peppered flesh and ate him.

Close Call at Flat Rock

My dad loved to dabble in politics - "dabble" being the key word, as he never enjoyed much success at it.

But Mark and another friend and I enjoyed some success from his efforts once during a Saturday hunting episode. We were teenagers.

It was a gorgeous autumn day. We had driven a few miles from home to the country to hunt on some friendly land. It was one of the steadily growing areas where hunting was restricted to shotguns. Not sure if we were after anything in particular, but I'm guessing rabbits mainly or possibly squirrels or crows or their ilk.

Regardless of what we thought we were hunting, our luck was zip. Not even a shot. We enjoyed our manly pursuit nonetheless, prowling gamely through the woods and pasture, our guns at the ready, expectations full to the brim with hope.

Come sunset, the hope had curdled. We sloughed back to our car and stood around, peering intently at anything within range that seemed to be moving. A dead leaf or two waved in the breeze of approaching dusk, but nothing with blood in its veins appeared.

So, with ammo at reasonable prices in those days, we decided to empty our shotguns by firing off each gun's chambered shell or two instead of removing them to hunt another day. There was a huge, plateau-shaped rock upon which we climbed, one at a time, to execute this impromptu ritual conclusion to our unproductive hunt. We aimed at the clouds.

"Boom!" "Boom! Boom!" "Boom"

We returned to the car and dispiritedly sheathed our guns. Right about then, the game warden's dark green car crunched across the gravel road, appearing out of nowhere, and blocked our exit.

Fully uniformed, including his revolver and Smokey the Bear hard-brimmed hat, the warden eased out of his car and swaggered over to ours. No, he didn't say, "You inna heapa trouble, boys," but we sensed that this is what he was thinking.

He told us it was after the legal hours to hunt. We said we knew that, and that this is why we were no longer hunting. He said, but you fired your guns. We did not deny this, and explained that we were simply wasting ammunition by shooting at the sky.

He stared at us awhile, then shifted his gaze to the ground around us, presumably looking for evidence - feathers, blood, rabbit hair, something incriminating.

"I've been watching you since you arrived," he said, startling us in a new, queasy way.

"We didn't see you," one of us croaked back.

"I was in that field," he said, pointing at a stand of yellowed cornstalks across the road, "watching you through binoculars."

I imagine the three of us immediately began scrolling through our memories of the past several hours, wondering what the hell we might have done or said - assuming the guy could read lips - that could get us into a heapa trouble. I know I did. I also experienced flashbacks of movie scenes involving potbellied southern sheriffs finding any excuse under the setting sun to put whomever they wished on a chain gang forever and ever.

"Yikes," I'm sure bubbled up somewhere inside my head - if, that is, my vocabulary included the word "yikes" in those days. If not, the spirit of "yikes" certainly bubbled up and floated around awhile.

We knew who the warden was. He was notorious locally for being a strict by-the-book prick, who reputedly had busted his brother-in-law moments after enjoying Thanksgiving dinner the warden's sister had prepared including some ducks her husband had shot out of season.

We knew this jackass wouldn't hesitate to write us up - meaning he could then seize our guns and keep them - if he found anything, any microscopic iota of violation any of us might have committed, inadvertently or otherwise. Advertently?

So far as we knew, he hadn't yet found anything, but I wondered if he was the sort of cop who would kick out a taillight in order to justify an arrest if he really wanted an arrest. And after sitting in a cornfield all afternoon watching three teenage boys through binoculars, you had to figure he'd want to find some way, any little way, to justify the effort.

"Open your trunk," he ordered, undoubtedly figuring he had us cold now, that if he could find anything in there that might be construed as illegal, he could write us up. Teenage boys? Of course, there would be *something* compromising in the trunk. He'd watched enough Dobie Gillis to know the likelihood of evidence being in there: a six-pack, girlie magazines, a body.

Marijuana was unknown to us back then. Only the migrants who came from Mexico to work in the canning factory knew about "funny cigarettes."

We'd come in my dad's car, so I opened the trunk, wondering myself what might be inside that could incriminate us with this desperately cynical cop.

What we all saw were some campaign posters from my dad's most recent unsuccessful campaign for public office. A judgeship or a state senate primary, come to mind. Whatever it was, he'd been smacked down by the voters because he was an awful campaigner (I was his campaign manager) and he never did anything to curry party support or raise money.

We all looked at each other. Ideas were forming. The game warden, studying one of the posters he'd plucked from the trunk, muttered something like, "Is this your dad?" He'd forgotten which one of us had the same last name, but he evidently remembered having seen that name recently.

One of my friends seized the moment. "Oh, yeah! That's his father!" He pointed at me. I nodded, feeling squirmy, but gradually sensing that we just might have passed some sort of crisis apex.

We had. The warden muttered some more words, finishing up with an admonition to obey the laws, etc. etc. He gave us our hunting licenses back, shuffled to his car, got in, backed out and drove away. Even his car looked disappointed.

Stump Shot

The greatest shot I ever witnessed was fired by my friend Mark. It was what we called a pot shot, the kind the good guys in comic books could do when I was a kid, whipping out a six-gun and snapping off a shot from the hip that zings the gun out of the bad guy's hand without hurting him. The Lone Ranger and Tonto could do it, Hopalong Cassidy did it and so did Roy Rogers, Gene Autry, Tom Mix and the Cisco Kid. Mark didn't shoot from the hip and his shot didn't zing a gun out of anybody's hand, but had the red-winged blackbird that was threatening us been holding one I've no doubt Mark's shot would have done just that. It was one of those shots you get, if you're lucky and not a government operative or Western entertainer who shoots thousands of rounds at targets every day, only once in a lifetime. If you're one of those guys and you're lucky, you might make a shot like Mark's two or three times in your prime. It was a shooter's hole-in-one.

Mark made the shot during one of our many stump sessions. The stump. I never took a photograph of it, and it's been so long since I've seen it – maybe 50 years – that it has metamorphosed in my imagination as something approaching myth. I see it now as a craggy gray thing about six feet tall with a waist-high diameter about a foot shy of that and losing another foot tapering upward. I see it as a miniature Devil's Tower about the size of the one Richard Dreyfus built in his bathtub in

Close Encounters. It was the place I did most of my early shooting, where I learned to become comfortable and fairly proficient handling firearms.

My initial exposure to shooting came as a Boy Scout during my several week-long summer adventures at Camp Tichora on Green Lake in south-central Wisconsin. Wait...let me back up a step. The first was at a place in Milwaukee my parents called The Arcade, which as I recall was probably one of the first indoor malls in Wisconsin and perhaps the Western Hemisphere. Likely the only reason I remember The Arcade is because among its tiny shops and stalls was a small shooting gallery, same as those at fairs and carnivals.

I wish my memory would serve up more details about the very first shot I ever fired out of one of those sleek air-powered rifles that were connected by a pneumatic tube to the booth counter. I remember less of what I did than of what happened to me. That first firing *crack* when I pulled the trigger opened some valve in my endocrine system that loosed a shot of a hormonal chemical that communed with an enzyme in my limbic infrastructure changing me, for better or worse, but changing me indeed. For life. I suspected even then the likelihood was slim I'd ever become a real cowboy, but with that rifle in my hands, popping at the steel squirrels and rabbits moving along a conveyor at the back of the stall, hearing the *crack* of my shot and the instantaneous *dink* of a hit and seeing the target disappear, I was at that moment Hoppy, Gene, Roy, Cisco Tom, Tonto and Ranger Reid all wrapped in one skin.

The Camp Tichora range had a format more martial than Western. We walked down a winding path from our cabins through the woods to a formal shooting range, with benches and target frames mounted against a sandy berm at least twenty feet high. Other than the Order of the Arrow ceremony the last night of camp, our several range trips were the most solemn of our week's activities. We were shooting real bullets, many of us for the first time in our lives. There was none of the giggling, grab-assing tomfoolery that made up most of the rest of our Tichora experience. The range officers were military in bearing and in the drill they imposed without waver. I remember only one joke that ever emerged from those riveting range sessions. It got a laugh just the first time, but was uttered by at least one participant ever after as a response to the order, once the targets were set and the shooters in place, locked and loaded: "Fire at will."

"Poor Will," came the murmured echo.

"Poor damn bird," was one of my mental responses at the stump years later when Mark made his shot. My vocal reaction was more like, "Damn, Mark, that was a helluva shot! Damn bird." We'd been plinking, shooting at pop and beer cans jammed into the stump's niches and crannies. I had my .22 caliber Mossberg carbine, the one with the front stock that folded down so I could hold it as if it were a Thompson submachinegun. Mark had a Crossman air rifle that shot a lead pellet. If he pumped the cylinder enough times the gun's piston would hurl that pellet at nearly the same velocity as my .22.
Evidently a red-winged blackbird had a nest nearby. The stump sat between a pasture and a mowed stretch that served as an

airfield for the several planes, including my dad's, that were hangared there. Actually the stump was just this side of the fence separating the properties. We were careful never to endanger the cows that would come lumbering up until the shooting started. Then, annoyed by the noise, they'd stare at us a minute or two, chewing lazily on their cuds, and lumber off into the nearby trees. This is probably where the bird's nest was, and the birds were perhaps more than just annoyed. They might well have worried we would miss our target and hit something more vital to their interests.

Thus, one of them decided to annoy us back, flying over our heads, circling and hurling down upon us a cacophony of scolding, cursing and who knows what else. And it did annoy us. Enough that we couldn't concentrate on our cans to hit them with the consistency we expected. We flung expletives in its direction, waved our guns in the air and shouted, threw things at it, sticks, stones, but nothing we employed cowed it in the least as it continued to screech and swirl perhaps twenty feet above our heads. I fired my .22 in the air to scare it. No dice. Eventually, his patience expired, Mark looked up and studied the bird a moment. Then, holding the rifle stock firmly against his shoulder, he carefully raised the barrel so it pointed straight up. At this angle the sound of a shot coming from the barrel, its sonic waves dispersing toward the sky, was muffled to a soft *pop*. But I heard it and I saw the bird's circling cease, as did its screech as the stubborn sentinel plummeted straight to the ground, dead at Mark's feet.

"Damn," was the word.

Jedi Pee Control

It's all in the mind. Easy to say and easy to tell oneself when one dabbles in Eastern mystical disciplines, such as concentrating on holding one's breath or contemplating a walk across glowing coals.

Those are voluntary exercises, easily abandoned if one is ill-motivated or too timid to pursue them. I've been thinking about this topic since watching Men Who Stare at Goats on Netflix recently at home. I had to pee, and almost panicked when I couldn't find the remote to pause the movie until I could take care of business. I found it in the nick of time.

But later, perhaps a day later, I got to wondering how goat-starer Lyn Cassady, the George Clooney character, would have handled my little emergency. Or even Clooney himself, assuming he had to learn something about mind control so he could look natural as his Cassady character made clouds move and goats drop dead just by staring at them. Clooney probably could have willed his bladder to settle down and wait for the damned movie to end. And it would have, the bladder.

Maybe not so easy if Clooney had the hair-trigger bladder alarm that some guys develop when they get to be my age. Lyn Cassady could have done it with barely a passing notion, but me? That's what got me to wondering. Could I control my overzealous bladder alarm with the same Jedi methods invented by novelist Kevin Anderson, which inspired the young U.S. elite Army officers whose theories, we are told, were incorporated into the successful strategy Stormin' Norman Schwarzkopf used to seriously whup Saddam Hussein's seriously overestimated forces in the First Gulf War?

If they worked in Kuwait, could they enable me to wait without groaning and squinching my face and pressing my knees together whilst hunting desperately for an escape to somewhere, anywhere where I could preempt an impending urinary disaster in a social setting, or even alone? I didn't wish to resort to *Flomax*, as I already take too damned many pills, and I damned sure was not about to get into *Depends* - yet.

The alternative was to reason my way out of the overpowering urges to pee. And I am not exaggerating the tiniest bit by using the often abused term "overpowering." I had several weapons - all of them mental - on my side. I knew that in most cases the bladder alarm was false, triggered by a notion that was magnified many-fold by the slightest pressure of actual urine in the bladder. I knew that the sense of pressure could not be merely poo-pooed away, that even a modicum of pee would take advantage of the panic the alarm sets off and try to squirt its way out so as not to be blamed for a bursting bladder. I knew this because it had done so on various occasions.

There was considerable trial and error involved in developing my Jedi strategy. Pride was key. You're a Jedi, I told myself. Jedis do not wet their pants unnecessarily. It helped. Believe me. Eventually I came to recognize that these surges of faux pressure were temporary, so long as I did not succumb to panic. The pressure grew relentlessly if I scrambled to get to a place where I could relieve it. If I knew I simply could not, depending on where I was or who I was with, the surges weren't nearly so bad. So, at home, where these events are always the worst, I tried casually walking past the toilet, telling myself: it's just a phony surge and it won't last long, you're a Jedi and you had goddam better not wet your pants, etc.

It worked. It works, mostly. What I need to be careful of now is not to get too cocky (yeah yeah) and let the bladder pool build up to the extent that the pressure is real and not to be denied by tricks of a mere mind. A sort of boy-who-cried-wolf ethic has inserted itself into my calculations.

I'm game. What the hell, I'm a Jedi.

Book on Books

After 44 years I still don't know what it was about me that George Whitman didn't like, if anything. It might have been my haircut. He might have thought I was a CIA agent. I was an American on leave from the Army and Whitman's Communist convictions were causing him official problems in the mid-1960s. The French government even shut him down for a while in 1968 accusing him of housing Communists during the May student riots in Paris, which he was.

I met him in May 1966. We were never introduced, but I spoke with him one time at the front desk of his bookstore. Our conversation went something like this: "Excuse me, do you have anything by Rousseau?" I had to repeat this once or twice, as Whitman seemed absorbed by something, either something on his desk or in his mind. Eventually he turned his head, barely enough to look at me. His face conveyed annoyance, if not incipient contempt.

"What did you say?" From the loaded indifference in his voice he might have been on the verge of telling me to get the hell out of his sight. I repeated my question. My mistake, I soon learned, was in mispronouncing "Rousseau," probably misplacing the accent or even dragging the esses to sound like zees. He made me repeat my blunder another time or two before correcting me, his voice now curled in a sneer. When I nodded yes, he growled no, stared hard at me a moment longer and then turned back to whatever had been occupying his attention.

What surely clinched the unfavorable impression he'd evidently already formed of me was the book I finally purchased. It was a paperback copy of Dashiell Hammett's *The Maltese Falcon*. Not a bad choice for a detective novel, but, as I was to learn just the other day, Whitman has a low opinion of the genre. Other than to take my money and put the famous Shakespeare and Co. stamp in my purchased books, he never bothered to even glance at me again on my numerous successive visits his store.

Stationed in West Germany I'd saved up my leave time and spent it all in Paris - two or three weeks. A friend who had just returned from the City of Light raved about the famous bookstore on the Left Bank facing Notre Dame. It was named after the literary hangout for Lost Generation expatriots in the 1920s and '30s run by Sylvia Beach. Her store had achieved international acclaim for publishing James Joyce's *Ulysses* and was personally liberated from the Nazis by Ernest Hemingway. Whitman's successor to the legendary Beach bookstore had won recognition by a new generation of young literati, with luminaries such as Ginsberg, Corso, Kerouac and Ferlinghetti frequenting the place, sleeping, writing and working there occasionally and giving readings. Whitman even published Ginsberg's *Howl*, when no one else would touch the cutting-edge poem that became an anthem for the Beat Generation.

During his sojourn in Paris my literary Army buddy had gotten to know a young writer Whitman befriended after learning the man was sleeping under a bridge over the Seine. The writer was now living and writing at the bookstore. Sounded like my kind of place. Even after the cold reception I got from Whitman, I couldn't stay away, seduced by its exotic ambience.

I have been seduced anew by Jeremy Mercer's charming memoir of the months he spent in Paris in 1999 living at Shakespeare and Co. Mercer ended up at the bookstore after fleeing to Paris from Ottawa where he'd been a crime reporter and had seriously pissed off an ex-convict who vowed revenge. Mercer's book, *Time Was Soft There*, brought back memories and dreams from my time in Paris and shed some light on the personality of George Whitman, the man I'd annoyed or worried more than four decades earlier.

Whitman, it seems, continued throughout the years to be suspicious of Americans, considering anyone he didn't know to be a potential CIA agent. He's a moody man and can be grumpy and hostile without warning, and he loathes detective mysteries.

A Google search indicates Whitman is pushing 100 years of age but is still kicking, although he has turned over the Shakespeare and Co. keys to his daughter, Sylvia.

I'm not certain if I've ever learned how to correctly pronounce Rousseau.

Gun With No Name
(fiction)

It would be good to describe the landscape and weather as we strode toward the place where it would happen, whether there were stalwart sycamores to block a probing, merciless sun or if the sky hosted friendly clouds that slid past absorbing the celestial blaze. I can tell you it was horribly hot. This I knew from the sweat soaking through the Boss' back pocket, where I rode unholstered, butt down, muzzle cloaked by a handkerchief.

I'm neither apologizing nor complaining. The circumstances are inherent in my assignment. I might have gotten a more visible job, a more ceremonial one riding in a belt holster on the hip of some aging city detective or country sheriff. I'm good looking enough to ride out front, but I was made for serious stuff. This means working undercover as a hideout. I'm a J-frame Airweight .38 snubby. I may be small and seem inconsequential to some, but I'm the one that never gets left in the safe. I'm always on duty.

At first the Boss fussed over me a little, wiped off all the grease, swabbed out my barrel and carried me to the range in the factory box to try me out. He seemed surprised that I kicked him as much as I did with the +P loads he was using. We didn't stay long that first day. Before he took me out again he switched my rubber Hogue grips for a set of smooth African blackwood Spegel Boot Grips. For a moment I experienced a sensation of grandeur, a fleeting notion that maybe I'd be riding out front in a belt holster for all to see. I suppose it's possible that a slick Alessi Talon or Sparks Summer Special is on order and that my notion will come to pass some day, but if it does it will come as a surprise, as I quickly got past that flicker of vanity.

My only complaint is the lack of action. The Boss stopped shooting me, and I miss that. I get a lot of range time, but always butt down in the pocket. Rarely fired. Unseen and all but forgotten in a denim pouch, riding the recoil ripple as Esmeralda, his 1911A1 Series 70 belches through box after box of .45acp Blazers or Casper, his Kahr E-9, performs a similar exercise, though more shrill, with the 9mm Blazers. I was particularly annoyed at first when Clyde came along to the range. Clyde's a Taurus .22LR snubby. The Boss likes to tell folks at the range that Clyde -- he doesn't speak their names at the range -- is a good way to practice snubby handling because it's cheap. He never says it's because Clyde is less painful, but I know that's another reason for all his practice with wimpy .22s.

The names came out at the shop. Dickey's Outdoor Supplies. The Boss likes to hang out there. It has an old potbelly stove and some raggedy stuffed chairs and a couch. It's where the Old Stove Biding, Bitching and Bullshooting Forum holds its meetings. The Boss is clearly a leading member of this august organization.

"So what's Esmeralda up to now, Doc? She been bad?" The speaker was J.P. Dickey, shop owner and a two-time IDPA state champion. Dickey's is popular with handgunners for various reasons, not the least of which is its employment of the only certified gunsmith within 100 miles--or so I heard the Boss tell someone at the range once, without contradiction.

"New sights," said the Boss. "I'm thinking of carrying her. That rib's too damned heavy and I don't need adjustables." Thus I learned of Esmeralda, and soon the others. I was new then. He bought me at a gun show. I wondered at first if that was why he never mentioned me in the shop, because he hadn't bought me there. Eventually it became clear that he wouldn't mention me to anybody, anywhere. This realization brought with it a sense of relief. I had grown accustomed to being the hideout. I also experienced a rush of pride that I had become the Boss' real gun, the one he'd come to trust over all the others.

The Boss was some kind of doctor. I say was because I think he's mostly retired. The doctor part came to me from everyone calling him "Doc," and an occasional consultation with members of the Forum, advice on how to deal with ailments. The Forum members are pretty stoic, except for occasional complaints of arthritis, sore backs, failing eyesight and trick knees. The kind of complaints that could be used as excuses for not doing things and for lousy marksmanship. I haven't seen any of them yet, but I do believe the Forum is made up of mostly old farts. Grumpy as old farts are, I should note, but with just enough drollery in their bones to keep each other from falling asleep around the stove.

My favorites are Sam, who I think is a retired or nearly retired cop of some kind. Every now and then his "haw haw haw" bursts out unexpectedly, usually drawing some supporting chuckles from the others. Then there's "Judge," which is all anybody ever calls him, but who talks like he either is or was a judge or a lawyer who thinks he's a judge. I don't mean this last part derisively. He's not pompous, but his voice is always measured and calm, as if he thinks everything through carefully before speaking. "Sam," he might say after Sam has held forth about some local scofflaw that Sam has tried unsuccessfully to send "up the river" over a good part of his career, "You know you'd have been better off shooting him the first time you caught him" doing something or other -- stealing a car or having broken into somebody's house -- "Then you could have moved on to chasing some other ne'er-do-well, like Red Quinn, and saved us all a lot of frustration and wasted time." After a silence, during which I picture Sam fixing Judge with a smoldering glare, suddenly would come the well-earned "haw haw haw. Ne'er-do-well. Red Quinn. Haw haw..." etc.

The Boss is either divorced or widowed. Whichever, he never talks about his wife. He has a couple of grown kids, but barely keeps in touch with them. If there are grandchildren, they never come around. The Boss did have a girlfriend, Doris, and she was with him when it happened.

A walk in a park, I guess. Nothing planned. At least I don't remember any conversation leading up to it, but the Boss is never especially chatty. We rode in his car for awhile, then parked, got out and walked, strolled, I suppose is the better word. The terrain evidently was rather uneven, judging from the Boss' rolling gait, which I keenly felt. There was some friendly bumping of the two, and I noticed that often the Boss made sure his hand was between me and whatever part of her was bumping or getting bumped. I never heard him speak of guns with her, and I deduced from this that she was not a gun person. That made me curious as to why he spent as much time with her as he did. They got along, though, so far as I could tell. She had a nice laugh. Low and merry. She struck me as pretty easy going.

They were bantering in a kind of coded way, using, it seemed, as few words as possible, the words sounding happy, contented. The mood change was subtle at first, but it was abrupt and it quickly grew tense. It apparently started with a sense of danger that the Boss picked up on. His hand brushed my pocket, then patted it quickly and moved away. His gait stiffened and slowed. The first voice I heard was his, speaking quietly but distinctly. "Let me handle this. Stay back." He was giving an order, something I can't recall I'd heard him do before. There was a new tautness in his voice. A slight quaver. I had no doubt some kind of peril was near.

The new voices came into range an instant after the Boss told Doris to stay back. One had a whiny quality, which at first didn't strike me as menacing. Only when I recognized some of the words did I understand the trouble we'd just met. These were "pay" and "toll" and "mother" and "fucker," the last two slurred together into one word. It was the cruel, feral laughing of another, even higher pitched male voice that jolted me into condition red. From that point on I paid rapt attention to every word and nuance of the situation.

It seemed the Boss had frozen. His trembling was strange. It worried me. What worried me more was hearing Doris pleading with what I now knew were armed robbers.

"Please don't shoot us," she said in a prayerful tone. "Take everything we have, but please don't shoot us." From the Boss' sudden shift in balance I knew he was reaching out to her. Then, even more abruptly, there was a thump, and we reeled backward.

"I told you to freeze, motherfucker! Didn't I tell you to freeze? You disobeyed me, motherfucker. I ought to cap you ass, and you ole lady's too."

"Yeah, let's cap the motherfuckers," came the other, younger sounding voice. I wanna see that motherfucker's head blow apart. I wanna have my way with the ole lady first. OK, Bro? Then we shoot the shit out of both of 'em. OK?"

"That ole lady? She ugly, TJ. I be cutting off her titties first, if she got any," said the first punk. "Then I be cutting off the little wormy thing he tries to fuck her with. If he got one. Hee hee hee hee..."

By now Doris was quietly sobbing. As the Boss recovered his balance after being struck or shoved, his hand found its way back to the pocket where I restlessly nestled. Fingers reached in, and one of them hooked through my trigger guard, the way he had practiced drawing me. In the drill, his index finger snagged me up and out of the pocket, twirling me as soon as I was free so that my barrel was pointed forward, my grip in his palm. The handkerchief always came out at the same time, as it did now.

The Boss's quick movement getting me into position did not go unnoticed by the robbers. This was the critical moment -- could the Boss get me into position before the target realized what was happening?

"Hey, lookee," one of the voices almost shrieked. "He got a hanky. Awww, he gonna cry jus' like his ole lady. What a pussy. Hey, Bro, lookit the pussy cry…"

The Boss' trigger finger ended my apprehension of any voices at this point by squeezing off the first of my five rounds of 135-grain Speer Gold Dot +P hollow points, designed especially for snubbies at the request of the NYPD. I saw my first target clearly from under my handkerchief shroud. Moon face, mean squinting eyes and hair in a complicated tangle. The eyes opened very wide very quickly as the copper-jacketed slug raced toward them at 860 feet per second about four feet away. It hit one of the eyes, creating a hydraulic effect that released a misty cloud of blood, brain fluid and bits of eye as my second bullet caught the robber just under his chin.

Boss then pivoted slightly and lined me up on the chest below another head, this one shiny bald with a face already wide with alarm. The creep, standing a couple of feet further back, was starting to raise some sort of Glock, holding it sideways, when my last three rounds interfered with his plan. The bullets grouped nicely within a four-inch circle in the middle of a black tee shirt inscribed in chalky white with some gibberish and an obscene symbol. Were I the sighing type, I'd have let out some anxious air as the white design burst into a glistening, viscous red blossom while its bearer headed to Earth for the final landing.

The Boss and Doris sat in the grass, entwined in each others arms, murmuring. The Boss had pushed my cylinder open and set me on the ground to the side. The police arrived within minutes and took me into custody.

I eventually made it back to the Boss, but things were a bit different. I never saw Doris again or heard her voice. The last words I heard from her came right after the police arrived. "Is that your gun?" she said to the Boss, shuddering as a uniformed officer picked me up by the muzzle.

"Yes," said the Boss.

"You mean you've been carrying a gun all the time I've been with you?"

"Yes, Doris."

"But...but don't you think you should have told me you were carrying a gun when we were together?"

"Maybe so, but I know you dislike them. I didn't want you to worry."

A long silence followed. She broke it, with a voice strangely cold and distant.

"I guess I don't really know you," she said. She had moved away from him in the grass

Broken Field Dreaming

Taking terrible license with fly fisherman Norman Maclean, I would say the line between football and religion for me is more of an ellipsis. My religion is too undisciplined to define, and football is...well, I've always loved it, but was good at it for only two moments. Flukes each, as I was too slow, clumsy and puny to be able ever to laugh condescendingly at that pathetic photo of a malnourished Richard Nixon in his Whittier football togs. Even in shoulder pads Nixon didn't look like a football player, and he wasn't. I didn't either, and wasn't, except for those two fine plays.

Both were during touch games half a century ago. Only the cusps of those triumphant moments are indelible. The time my leap and reach were accidentally perfect and I snagged an interception in  the net of my outstretched fingers. I may have run for a touchdown afterward, so surprised would have been the other team in our pickup game. If so, the scoring was anticlimactic enough to have faded from memory. It's the catch that lives, that hang-time catch alone, arcing over the decades. It still lights in me the endorphinous glow that is the reward of sublimely perfect accomplishment.

Years later it was the perfect pass I threw in another pickup game – one among mostly strangers – that smolders yet in my private hall of glory. My team, hastily picked to kill time between rehearsals of the University of Wisconsin Marching Band, in which I played cornet, was having trouble finding a quarterback. We passed the job around after each series of downs in the hope someone with a modicum of skill might emerge. When it came my turn, I threw it. The perfect pass. Lofted it easily, long.

I can still see the ballistic spiral as the ball rocketed downfield from my hand toward the running receiver with just enough velocity to carry it over his head and into his hands. From where I stood, maybe fifteen yards away it appeared to be an effortless catch. He may have scored, but I don't think so. I'd have levitated. What I'll never forget is the instantaneous electric charge the play sent through us all on the Field House parking lot. The faces and postures of the players on my team reached to me with a conspiratorial excitement the likes of which previously I'd only have imagined. Worry visibly waxed among our opponents. I savored their discontent.

The only other recollection I have of that game is of the equally rapid plunge back to my initial obscurity and beyond, to a forlorn disappointment among my teammates. The specific remaining passes I threw before I was replaced elude me. I know only that they were no good, and one may have been intercepted. I know irrefutably that someone else seized the quarterback job for the next play series. I vaguely recall we found someone who could throw well consistently. I have no clue who won.

Nestled between these two episodes of splendor also live the only four scenes I retain in visual memory from playing high school football. In the one most vivid I'm standing, unhindered by any blockers a few steps away from the opposing quarterback. This was one of my first plays in an actual game. The quarterback looked at me as I looked at him, but he looked frail and scared. I felt like a giant, as if I could easily dash him to the ground. Instead I stared at him, overwhelmed by the sheer sensation that I was in a real football game and could make a big play – me, puny little me, who as a child had set up an obstacle course of chairs throughout the house to practice "broken-field running," and who had gotten hysterical after seriously cutting my right hand, afraid I would never be able to play quarterback, who had learned to pray at the radio during Packer and Badger games, knowing all the players' names and dreaming, dreaming, sickly, fragile, awkward kid that I was, that someday I would be a real football player, now suddenly *was* a football player.

Years later a scene in James Jones's *The Thin Red Line*, where the protagonist stands eye-to-eye with his first enemy soldier, resonated familiarly with me. Although I had never been in war, and carried only a romantic sense of what it must be like, I understood when Jones's character killed the other soldier and found the act ugly. It disappointed me, but I knew what he felt. The quarterback threw his pass untouched by me, because at that instant, during a hesitation of no more than a fraction of a second, I was identifying as much with his as my own role.

I think that high school game was the only one I suited up for, being also in the band, which, in the tangle of my adolescent values, took a begrudged priority over practically everything else. This game was also Dad's Night. It was my senior year, my last chance to play official tackle football and I'd been able to persuade my fearful parents that I was rugged enough at last to do so. At 125 pounds, I wasn't, but then neither was our team. A Madison sportswriter, describing one of our games, wrote that our quarterback was the only member of the team who could realistically be considered a football player. The writer exaggerated, but there was no question we were outclassed, scoring a total of six points all season, which set a record of embarrassment for our school that has yet to be matched.

Did I make contact in that game? Oh, yes. On probably the very next play, following the one in which I watched the opposing quarterback throw his pass unmolested, the blocker who should have taken me out on that play did so now. Except that when we collided I inadvertently injured his groin. I remember feeling astounded that I was responsible for the heap of groaning enemy football player curled up on the ground. He whacked hell out of me on the very next play, although I don't recall feeling any pain or being aware of anything especially unpleasant. He probably swung at me, however, because the referee called an unsportsmanlike conduct penalty on him, which moved his team back fifteen yards, resulting possibly in the most positive yardage for us in the entire game.

Reading *Paper Lion* years afterward it occurred to me that maybe I'd done Plimpton first.

One might think someone who loved the game despite being poor football material himself might at least be a discriminating fan. I wasn't. Not by today's standards, anyway. I grew up listening to games on the radio. There was one announcer. No color man to interrupt action talk with endless trivia or instant analyses. Just the one announcer, who basically followed the ball, revealing who had it and what he was doing, or what was being done to him.

Fred Gage's emotion-whipped tenor was the voice of the Wisconsin Badgers. "Coatta's back to pass," he'd shriek. "He's looking downfield! He dodges one tackler! Another! He throws! It's a long, long, long pass! Beautiful pass! Jim Temp has it!! Big Jim Temp caught the ball! He's going all the way! He's down to the fifteen, the ten, the five...TOUCHDOWN BADGERS!!!"

My dad took me to a few Wisconsin games, no more than one a year. These were trips to Mecca. Among my loveliest memories will ever be the heart-quickening glimpses of a looming Camp Randall stadium as we walked toward it among the garishly bedecked student and alumni tribesmen, all streaming in the same direction, excitement building with each step. Once in awhile we'd be late, and we'd hear the sudden roars from within the oval stadium in response to plays in a game already started. We never had advance tickets, but never had a problem buying a couple near the gate from someone who had extras. My dad would have been outraged had the price been anything more than what was printed on the tickets, so I know we were never scalped.

Once inside the stadium the excitement peaked in a way of nothing else I've ever experienced. Even so I was always slightly disillusioned with what I saw on the field. The action never quite lived up to the games Fred Gage described in my imagination, reinforced next morning by the sequential photos of key plays in the Milwaukee Journal. I would study those photos and try to remember how Gage had described the particular play they depicted, seeking nuances of body angle and contortion, from frame to frame, trying to understand what had been going through the players' minds, how the plays had actually looked. The photos were icons.

These days I watch TV games sporadically, depending on who's playing. Only with Wisconsin and Green Bay games does the old fire return, but I prefer to watch them alone. Too many watchers today are too analytical for my taste. The unrestrained passion is missing. I really could care less whether someone's switching from zone to man coverage or back again, or who might be clipping, trapping, holding or pulling. I'm a Fred Gage kind of watcher. The excitement for me is the ball – where it is, who has it and what he's doing or what's being done to him. I shout, stomp, curse and bellow. I feel awful when my team loses and terrific when we win. Yeah...we. I get a little superstitious at these times, and I say this not just to set up my last anecdote, although it surely does.

My most memorable year as a fan was also the most memorable year for my beloved Packers. It was 1967 and their greatest game of the year came on the last day of the year. It has come to be known as the Ice Bowl. The game concluded with a play of infarctional suspense, which I experienced in the room of Achal, a graduate engineering student from India and as tyrannical a leader of Green Bay Packer fans as was Vincent Lombardi, the

Packers' indomitable and inimitable coach, of the players themselves.

Achal, which was the only name any of us knew him by, was in such total control of our group of about a dozen students who lived in the rooming house on Mifflin Street that even though he trusted us to do nothing ritualistically incorrect to queer the outcome of a game were he to leave the room for any reason, there was only one time I recall that he actually left before the game had ended.

This was just before the Ice Bowl's horrific ultimate play.

"I cannot watch. Oh. My heart will stop. I cannot watch. Don't tell me. Don't tell me. Oh. My heart will stop. Don't tell me..."

Achal's cantillation rose in agony as he fled the room where the rest of us sat frozen in front of his small black-and-white TV. The wailing grew to a howl outside the room louder presumably to drown out what he might hear through the closed door. But the cry was so genuinely stricken that his roommate Rami rushed out to be with him. I, for one, felt a flash of empathy with Achal, an impulse to join him. Enduring suspense has never been my strong suit. But I remained with the rest. We sat in chairs Achal'd assigned each of us with the ardor of a deeply liturgical man. We sat in them during winning games. Not only sat, but leaned in certain ways that Achal reminded us of during certain crucial plays.

"You, Mat-yew, you sit this way!" He would demonstrate, slapping a hand on his own knee and jutting his chin forward at the proper angle. Those who were amused by his startlingly accurate impressions quickly learned to keep their amusement to themselves. Achal held us in line with the crisp arrogance of a sultan: "You shut up! Watch!" Same attitude when he addressed the TV screen. "Elijah's going to get the ball. GIVE ELIJAH THE BALL!!"

Achal was Hindu. When not in the grip of a game his demeanor was sweet as the milk-laden tea he supplied endlessly. "Hi, I am Achal. I like Green Bay Packers. Do...you...like, eh?" It was his standard introduction. Safe enough in Madison, where, he was quick to tell anyone who passed the initial test with a nodding smile, he was studying engineering so he could join his brother's business in Green Bay, where, by the way, Achal's wife lived and went to the home games with Mrs. Bart Starr. That's right. The sparkling eyes in Achal's beaming Buddha face examined each prospective friend intently during this monologue, as though hungry for the reflections of the childlike excitement the words renewed in him each time he said them. His was a simple charm impossible to resist. This is most likely why he always had the most housemates in his room each Sunday afternoon despite the color TV in another student's room upstairs.

Being a Achal regular was tougher than it might sound. He expected total loyalty and a willingness to accept Achal as final arbiter of how best to display that loyalty. This meant instant acquiescence to Achal's rules, which he issued intuitively from moment to moment.

True fans will submit to almost any demands to sustain a winning season. We were fascinated by the myth-spawning Lombardi, he of the Borgnine mug and Mafia don mien, whose tyranny players cringed from while loving him for his devotion. The alchemy was similar with Achal and his regulars. Discipline was rarely a problem. I can think of only once when Achal actually got tough.

A guest of one of the regulars announced before the start of a game that he was a fan of the team playing the Packers that day. Achal reacted instantly. "You are not Packer fan? Get out! Get out of my room! Get out!" There was no mistaking Achal's sincerity. He was clearly outraged. The guest looked around for some indication this was not serious or that Achal was merely a character whose idiosyncrasies the rest of us tolerated, but up to a point. Finding nothing encouraging, the guest relented, claiming he'd been joking. It was too late. He had spoiled his welcome. Under Achal's persistent barrage he left. For those of us who might have wondered, the answer was now beyond doubt. No loyalty jokes on game day.

Packer games in Achal's room were not parties. There might have been a little beer and some tobacco, but the events were indisputably a rite. Most of us in the Mifflin Street house were graduate students. Irrespective that some might have been church goers, for those who watched the games in Achal's room I suspect the several hours of identifying with a football team that mostly won in a weekly ordeal with so many variables as to be virtually unpredictable produced an emotional renewal deep enough to sustain us through another week of the academic joust.

Our experience as fans wasn't entirely vicarious if you allow that our devotion, which touched upon the mystical, made us participants in a metaphysical sense. There was a purity in Achal's room that beckoned to a spiritual realm. We never bet. On games or plays within games or anything else. No one spoke of this sense, excepting Achal's ordering where and how we would sit, but I know now that in some part of my heart I believed if we kept the faith that somehow in some infinitesimal way it could help spin the kind of psychic energy to positively affect the outcome of the game.

The moment when this near religious fervor was most apt to have counted was for the apocalyptic play whose imminence sent our leader chanting into the hall outside his room in fear for his very life. There he would remain, voicing his anguish until we signaled either our deliverance or else had absorbed for him the awful initial blow of catastrophe.

Much was at stake on this climactic play. We knew a touchdown would give the Packers a third straight National Football League championship and their second victory for that title over the Dallas Cowboys. We knew it was cold. So cold the playing arena, Lambeau Field in Green Bay, was a windy eighteen below zero – a record low there for a Dec. 31 – when the two teams crouched for that deciding play in the shade of a scoreboard at Dallas's end of the of the field. It was so cold several players suffered frostbite and all of them might have done better wearing ice skates. Their cleated shoes skittered uselessly most of the time on the frozen turf. So cold league officials had consulted physicians to help them decide whether to allow the game to be played.

The deciding play was the culmination of an afternoon of furious combat, albeit tickled at times with comic relief for those inside the action. Such was the nearly deciding play when a Packer known as "Gilly" fooled a Cowboy named Lilly into stepping the wrong way, which allowed a former "Eli" to carry the ball to the Dallas three-yard line. One play later Green Bay moved the ball to the one-yard line for a first down. This meant the Packers, behind 17-14, now had four chances to carry the ball one yard to score six points and win the championship.

Normally a situation like this was about as certain for Lombardi's Packers as Arnold Palmer with a six-inch putt. Stretching the metaphor, the Packers were facing the kind of complication Palmer might have had putting while perched on a skateboard and wearing mittens. Fumbles, missteps and pratfalls had given this game an air of Ringlingesque. The gut-squeezing goofiness persisted for the next two plays, with the slipping ball carrier's feet getting him down to only the one-foot line.

Complication suddenly loomed large. Technically Green Bay had two plays remaining. But with a total of just 16 seconds remaining in the game, if the next try also failed to cross the goal line the clock likely would run out before another play could be run. Green Bay had used up all but its final allotted time-out. A field goal would give the Packers three points to tie the game, but even kicking the ball through the goal posts at this range was not a given today. Besides, going for a tie was not the Lombardi way, and more besides, it was too cold to continue the game in overtime, which is what would have happened had a field goal been kicked.

There was some poetic justice in this dilemma for the Packers. In the championship match the previous year they had foiled a Dallas win in the final seconds with an impenetrable goal-line stand. We in Achal's room remembered this. What none of us knew, what would have sent the rest of us into the hall with the stricken Achal had we known, was that the upcoming play could be the final one for Lombardi as coach of the Packers. Only Lombardi knew at this moment that he planned to retire after the season.

The onus of deciding what to do that would either gild the legend of Lombardi and his Packers or coat it with bronze fell upon a man who once again was obliged to live up to his name: Starr.

Born Bryan Bartlett Starr, he became, in his universe, just plain Bart. Now an able offensive field commander, he'd been a late bloomer as a professional quarterback following a couple of pretty good seasons at the University of Alabama. His pro career was sputtering, as were the Packers, when Lombardi took over as coach in 1959.

His players have said Lombardi was a genius at motivating them to play to the peak of their potential. Starr was his brightest example, developing under Lombardi into a quarterback so poised and precise he appeared quintessential leading a team that within eight years was as close to perfect as a football team could possibly be. They lost a game now and then, as the very best football teams do. If football builds character, as its defenders contend, learning to lose gracefully is an important part of the lesson.

At the professional level, from which a Lombardi quote has become the maxim "Winning isn't everything, it's the only thing" and where the coach summed up one of his motivational approaches with, "If you aren't fired with enthusiasm you'll be fired with enthusiasm," losing, in order to serve a strategy of ultimate triumph within the broader measure of a playing season, must fulfill at least two interdependent needs: the education to enable you next time around to best whatever problems the other team threw at you, and the slap to prompt your enthusiasm to do it.

The 1967 Packers had four losing slaps and one tie in fifteen games going into the Ice Bowl. The Cowboys had been slapped five times in their fifteen games. Of interest in the dynamics losing may contribute to a team's momentum, Green Bay and Dallas each lost its last game of the regular season, both in close games, then went on to win handily in their playoff games. During the regular season the same two teams – Baltimore and Los Angeles – beat Green Bay and Dallas. The Packers redeemed their Dec. 9 loss to the Rams by whipping them two weeks later, a week before the Ice Bowl, after being whipped themselves by the Pittsburgh Steelers in between.

Up and down, down and up. Willy nilly, it seems, but there is pacing at work. Some games, because of the histories of the teams, fortunes of the week or the season, mental and physical states of the moment, simply carry more import for some players. Sometimes one player can make the difference, either in a crucial play or, if he's a leader, with the team's spark. Starr.

The only criticism ever aired of Bart Starr as Green Bay's quarterback was that he wasn't creative, that he functioned as a robot whose buttons were pushed by Lombardi. This criticism didn't come from Packers but from observers of the Packers. The men who played with Starr knew better, told stories of Starr's insisting on being allowed to run the team on the field and of instilling such confidence in fellow players in his doing so that an illusion of invincibility prevailed among them even when they appeared to be losing, as now.

Starr decided on a play. He knew it quite possibly could be the team's final play of the season or it could lift them into legend. He didn't have to, but, using the team's final time-out, Starr ran to the sideline to tell Lombardi what he wanted to do. Starr knew his boss well enough not to suggest a field-goal attempt. Even the fans knew Lombardi that well. No, the Pack would go for six points. The only question was how. The options: pass or run. Starr was a hurler of pinpoint accuracy, but the day was no day for passing a football. It was tricky enough holding onto the ball just standing still. Thus the ball would have to be carried, which opened up a new set of questions: who and where?

For the record, Lombardi approved Starr's call, joking afterward that he didn't want to keep the fans in the stands shivering any longer than necessary. Starr trotted back onto the field and into the huddle. He announced what the play would be, which told his teammates where the ball carrier would hit the Dallas line. Ordinarily with the play he called, the Yalie, fullback Chuck Mercein, would be the carrier. Starr never said otherwise, but he'd decided the carrier this time would be himself. If his teammates didn't know, they couldn't inadvertently signal to the Dallas players by a glance or a slight tilt of body or limb. Inadvertently signaling in such ways and reading of inadvertent signals between opposing players contribute much to the split-second tactical jockeying that can spring a runner for a long gain, open a pass receiver downfield or get the ball stuffed by the defense for lost yardage or worse.

Starr's play was called a wedge. It was a simple-simon play intended to do just what its name said it should do, drive a wedge of maniacally ferocious men with the ball carrier behind them through a wall of maniacally ferocious men trying to stop them. The distance needed this time was about twelve inches. Tough enough under normal conditions, but the Dallas wall in the last two plays had stopped Green Bay's toughest runner each attempt. The first effort failed after a Green Bay lineman flubbed his block. It was the same lineman, Jerry Kramer, who had to get it right this time for Starr to be able to score. Kramer at 31 was an old man in the game, nearing the end of his playing career. He was so scarred from injuries his teammates called him "Zipper." Kramer lined up across from a huge, quick, strong, considerably younger man, Jethro Pugh, who had been giving Kramer trouble all day, as had another Dallas defender, Willie Townes, who was lining up beside Pugh.

Kramer crouched beside his center, Ken Bowman, from whom Starr would take the ball as he launched the play. To get some traction Kramer dug the cleats of his right shoe into the frozen turf. His plan was to hit Pugh so quickly Pugh wouldn't be able to react in time to stop the ball carrier. Bowman would hit Pugh too. The two Packers gambled the play would be over before Townes could get to the ball. Starr leaned against Bowman's buttocks, his hands reaching down between the center's thighs. Starr called out some signals. When he reached a prearranged count, Bowman snapped the ball up into Starr's hands, then shoved off and lunged at Pugh, charging into the monster Cowboy an instant after Kramer. Hit with their combined weight of close to five hundred pounds of hurtling muscle and bone, Pugh went down. The play was over so fast it had to be studied with the new TV phenomenon "instant replay" to fully appreciate what happened.

While Jethro Pugh was toppling, Starr staggered a couple of steps forward with only Townes and a third Cowboy, Chuck Howley, close enough to threaten. Townes faltered, probably slipping, and Packer lineman Forrest Gregg threw his body across Howley's path, forcing the would-be tackler to leap over him, landing on Starr. But too late. Starr was on the ground, still hugging the ball, halfway over the goal line. Far enough. The game was over. Packers 21, Cowboys 17. During our jubilation Achal eased back into his room.

"...My heart will stop...What? We won? We won? We won! Oh! Oh! We won! Oh, here it is! Instant replay! Oh, look! Look! Oh, is it Bart Starr? It is Bart Starr! Oh! We won! We won..."

The Gray Ghost v. Football

Proposing herewith, that the game of football is unnecessarily brutal and dangerous to the health of its participants, we have the late Confederate Col. John Singleton Mosby, known throughout the tragic **War Between the States** by his unofficial *nom de guerre* "Gray Ghost."

Assuming the opposing position with its silence is the **University of Virginia**.

Now, lest anyone reading this account suspect that I am setting them up with a farcical irony such as ultimately revealing Mosby as a secret ninny who hid behind wartime propaganda designed to intimidate the enemy with false myth, perish the thought.

At least a dozen volumes have been published recounting Mosby's exploits as a guerrilla cavalry leader of exceptional courage and physical prowess on the battlefield. Many eyewitness accounts of his day-to-day heroism are part of our history.

 Following is but one of them, taken from James Ramage's biography of Mosby: *Gray Ghost*. Ramage relies on Mosby's report to his commander, Cavalry Gen. J.E.B. Stuart, who had sent Mosby and two other men to scout behind the Union lines along Virginia's Pamunkey River in the area of Hanover and King William counties. After leaving

one of the men to guard a Union supply wagon they'd captured and sending the other man to inform Stuart they'd spotted two supply schooners, Mosby rode on ahead.

He soon came upon a company of Pennsylvania cavalry, *mounted and drawn up in a line in the road.*

Mosby was alone and it was nearly sunset and his horse was exhausted from riding all day. He knew that if he turned to flee they could overtake him with their fresh horses. He halted in the middle of the road, purposefully drew his saber and turned in the saddle to wave it in the air, as if beckoning imaginary followers. "Come on, boys! Come on!" he shouted.

The Pennsylvania men did not wait to see who this Rebel might be addressing; they turned and quickly vanished.

After the war, Mosby returned to the law practice he'd started before enlisting in the Confederate Army, and eventually went to work for the U.S. Department of Justice. It was from his office in Washington, D.C. in 1909 that Mosby wrote to a friend in Richmond complaining about his lack of success in persuading his alma mater, the University of Virginia, to abolish football as an approved sport.

I do not think football should be tolerated where the youth of the country are supposed to be sent to be taught literature and humanity and science, he wrote in his letter to Thomas Pinckney Bryan, *The game seems to overshadow everything else at the University.*

I believe that cock-fighting is unlawful in Virginia. Why should better care be taken of a game chicken than a school boy?

He goes on to say, *If the teams were not school appendages and gave public exhibitions of skill as prize fighters, I would care nothing about them. The more that got killed the better. Football is only a polite term for prize fighting...it is notorious that football teams are largely composed of professional mercenaries who are hired to advertise their colleges.*

Gate money is the valuable consideration. There is no sentiment of Romance or Chivalry about them. The swords of the old Knights are rust.

In the interest of full disclosure it should be noted that Mosby did not participate in athletics when he attended the university. A scrawny, sickly youth of 19, he was, in fact, bullied by another student, George R. Turpin, a much larger man with a violent reputation. Mosby shot Turpin when the bully assaulted him outside the boarding house where Mosby was living.

Turpin lived and Mosby was convicted of unlawful shooting and sentenced to a year behind bars. While in jail he studied from law books brought to him by his prosecutor, who, after Mosby's release, took him into his practice and mentored him until the future Confederate hero received his own law license.

Fleeing Ibiza

"Everybody stand still. They've got guns."

Pete said it calmly, but with an unusual tension in his voice, and loudly enough so that we all could hear him. "We" were about two dozen strong at this point.

I'd finally gotten my degree, worked a year double shifting as a skycap and a security guard at the local airport in Madison, Wisconsin, and saved up for a Eurail pass and a couple of books of travelers checks, enough to bum around Europe in the summer of 1970.

Our group of wanderers had started aggregating in Barcelona, Spain, where college roommate Pete and I decided to take the slow boat to Ibiza. We'd not heard of Ibiza, the famous party place – one of the Mediterranean's Balearic islands – but had decided to visit at the prompting of someone we'd met while sipping wine in a local cafe. We were doing the Hemingway thing.

By the time our boat slid into its Ibiza berth we'd become friendly with about half a dozen others, with whom we set out to find a hotel. Alas, we soon learned there weren't any rooms. Tourist season had just begun, and everything was booked. Not to worry, said Klaus, a German we'd met on the boat, who was a regular Ibiza denizen. He led us through a brick-paved courtyard, down some stone steps and through a sort of alley/tunnel, under the buildings and out into the open air of the grassy bluff that sloped down to the sea from the ancient walls of what is known as the old city of Ibiza town, which had been built by the Phoenicians in 654 B.C.

The weather was comfortable. Klaus led us to a stretch of the bluff containing little hollows where we rolled out our sleeping bags. We cooked supper over campfires in front of these shallow caves before bedding down for the night.

Supper consisted of soup made with fresh vegetables and a skinny chicken that had cost us less than a dollar at a local market. Our beverage of choice was called herbas, an anise flavored, mildly alcoholic drink we paid pennies for at a local bodega. The bodega folks would fill a bottle from a large barrel that was filled routinely by locals who brewed their own stuff from herbs and sold it. Each day's blend, therefore, was a tad different from that of the prior day. We wouldn't have known, as the anise overpowered any nuance the nectar might have offered our unfamiliar palates.

Each night we were guarded by the wild dog that had adopted our particular cave, the price being a handout or two or three from our supper. Klaus explained that the dogs hanging out around the caves were indigenous to the island, unable to survive anywhere else. Yellowish tan and skinny, resembling a blue tick hound, they were friendly and loyal.

Not necessarily loyal to us, though, as we began to suspect one morning after spending several days and nights in this idyllic spot. One of the high points was waking each morning to watch the sun rise over the sea down the bluff in front of us, warming our caves and welcoming us to a new day.

On the morning our welcome ran out, the dogs were nowhere to be found. Instead, men in black suits emerged out of the morning mist and began closing in on our position.

Pete had risen before us, and had climbed the bluff to pee and to check out the "fortress." He was the first to see the approaching men in black.

Evidently his alarm was compelling enough to alert the other cave dwellers, as they were all clustered near us by the time the black-suited men had us neatly surrounded. We outnumbered them two to one, but they had hands under their jackets and we didn't. I saw no gun, and I don't think Pete did, either, but none of us needed such a graphic representation to know we'd soon see guns if we didn't behave as if we knew what was under those jackets.

We saw no badges. I, for one, wondered if they were gangsters, that maybe they kept drugs or other contraband stashed in the caves. We tried various languages, but they seemed not to understand anything we said. Eventually one of them said a word we understood, which sounded something like "passports." We quickly surrendered our passports. Somehow our captors were able to communicate to us that we needed to be at police headquarters at noon. Then they left, without returning our passports.

We kept our appointment. We were herded into a large room where someone who spoke English called us out one at a time to exit through a different doorway than we'd entered. This led us into a garage, where another English-speaking cop had our passports neatly stacked on the fender of a car. When it was my turn, the cop handed me my passport along with an order: be off the island by sunset or face formal deportation. He emphasized that the word "deported" stamped on a passport was not good.

In a daze, we shuffled across the street to the port office and inquired about tickets to leave Ibiza. The very merry agent told us there was only one boat leaving that day, for the next island up – Majorca – and that the rate had doubled or tripled over the cost of coming here from Barcelona. Some of us paid, others stayed behind to try their luck. We who paid sailed away to catch a bullfight in Palma. We never saw the others again.

I Don't Think So, Mr. Guttman

My dad began morphing into Kasper Guttman at the Selective Service office in Portage, Wis. We'd driven there to appeal a notice I received lifting my student draft deferment after I flunked out of college for the third time. The notice said I'd be re-classified 1-A unless I could persuade the local draft board otherwise.

It was spring 1963. U.S. military involvement in Vietnam was growing. Our role was still classified as advisory, but more and more American troops and war materials were showing up in that distant land every day. I was more annoyed than worried. I didn't especially want to be a soldier, but the prospect of adventure had a vague attraction. My dad was dead set against my being drafted.

We'd talked a little about my strategy on the hour-long drive from home. Were I enrolled in a community college I might get to keep my deferment. Trouble was, I was tired of school. I had lousy study habits. I had graduated with honors from high school, but it was a small school and the coursework wasn't rigorous. I hadn't developed enough self-discipline to cope with the independence, academic demands and social distractions of a major university. Maybe I could handle a smaller college, something more like my high school.

"Are you enrolled?" The woman behind the desk was the only person in the small office. Her hair was gray, but she was no

77

sweet, cheek-pinching grandma. No smile, no friendly greeting, flat voice. All business, this bureaucrat.

"Umm..."

My dad took over. "Not yet," he said, "But he intends to apply as soon as possible." There was some question as to whether my academic status might prevent me from enrolling in any college. We hadn't looked into that yet.

The woman's eyes never left mine. She asked another question or two, and each time my dad responded before I could say a word. Finally, she turned from me and addressed my dad. "Who is the applicant here, you or him?" She motioned with her head back at me, her voice arched with sarcasm.

Our little session was over. My dad abruptly stood. "Thank you," he snapped, then, to me, "Let's go." We did.

Just outside the office, loudly enough so the woman could hear him through the glass door, my dad told me not to worry, that he had some kind of legal leverage over one of the draft board members. A slap in the face couldn't have hurt me more than those words. I was stunned, but not so much that I couldn't feel the unfamiliar emotion that was born at that moment somewhere

inside my heart. It started as a spark of disbelief and quickly burst into disillusionment. Despite the frailties I had come to see in my dad – and there was a fair bill of particulars, considering his lawyerly self-loathing arrogance – my sense of his personal honor had never been in doubt. Seeing him now in a Sydney Greenstreet role, the kind of wheeling dealing villain who did what he had to do to get what he wanted no matter how foul or who might get hurt, *The Maltese Falcon*'s Kasper Guttman, was my first unsentimental glimpse of the man I had once wanted to be.

We drove home in silence. Next day I told my mother I was going to enlist in the Army. That evening, my dad tried to talk me out of it, hurling the usual clichés about throwing my life away and how dare I do this to them. I didn't budge. Then he played his trump card.

"You realize your killing your mother with this, don't you? Your mother is dying a little every minute because of this."

My anger was more controlled than I believe it had ever been. It was hard and cold and determined. I looked at my mother, who sat in a separate chair next to his.

"Are you, Gert? Are you dying a little every minute because I've decided to join the Army?" Our eyes locked. Ordinarily she'd have glanced at her husband before answering a question so clearly defiant of his authority. Instead she smiled, shook her head slightly and murmured, "No."

Facing the BMG

The rumors started early our last week of training. We would be crawling over gravel and we should buy Kotex at the PX to pad our elbows and knees. Guys who didn't wear pads ended up scraped and bleeding, we'd heard. It was our final and toughest course. Word was, guys who didn't keep their heads down had gotten shot. The most riveting story was confirmed by Sgt. Loudon, the feisty little West Virginian who'd relieved Sgt. Mulligan as our drill sergeant about halfway through the eight-week course (we heard it was Mulligan's drinking, we found his boots, with his name and service number Magic-marked inside just like ours, in the trash, they were small boots, smaller than most of ours, which confused us because Mulligan had seemed a big man with a rough, John Wayne presence). It was Sgt. Loudon who actually spelled out for us what had happened to the unnamed private we'd heard had been killed on the night infiltration course some time back. He told it as if he personally had witnessed what had happened.

"He got a dear John letter that morning," said Loudon, his black-ice eyes freezing anyone who dared look into them with their own. "He was quiet the rest of the day. Kept to himself. Didn't talk to none of his buddies. That night he started across the course with his platoon and about halfway in he threw down his piece and got to his knees and then he stood straight up. It looked like he was trying to say something, but nobody could make out what, with all the noise from the TNT and the BMG and everything. The BMG cut him in two, right below the shoulders. He looked like a big balloon full of blood bursting. They shut the course down for the rest of the night."

We were all staring at Loudon's eyes now, all of us frozen stiff. Loudon gazed back at us awhile, glancing around the group, no expression on his face. Then he looked down, shook his head and stood up. "Keep your god dam head down out there," he shouted, his voice ragged with emotion. "I don't wanna hafta mop up what's left of you out there. Keep your god dam head down." He turned and walked off.

I don't think anyone bought Kotex. That rumor didn't have much punch and we knew there was the chance it was a joke. Neither I nor the other men in my platoon had any intention of being a goat, either in the checkout line or back at the barracks opening a big box of feminine napkins to hoots and snickers. We would risk the scrapes and the bleeding joints. Facing the BMG was another matter.

Browning Machine Gun, firing .30-06 rifle cartridges fed by a belt at around 500 a minute. Workhorse of the infantry squad in the previous three wars and thus far in Vietnam, gradually being retired for the more efficient M60, but still capable of cutting a man in half in a couple of seconds. I carried that picture in my head the rest of the week as the countdown marched relentlessly toward our rendezvous with...I tried not to think what.

It was mid-November 1963 and change was in the air. We were a week away from becoming government issue soldiers. A remote place called Vietnam was cropping up more and more in the news. President Kennedy, planning a trip to Dallas, had about one week left to live.

The highlight of our final week, leading up to the NIC (Night Infiltration Course) exercise, was the historic surrender of our M1 Garand rifles to a private dealer before being issued the new M14s. We spent all  day cleaning our M1s for some guy who would turn around and sell them at a profit. Would have made for some interesting investigative journalism had anybody at Fort Jackson known about such things back then. Main difference between the two rifles was in weight and caliber. The longer, heavier M1 had served our ground troops since WWII. It fired the same 30.06 cartridge as the BMG and the M1903 Springfield it replaced after WWI. The new rifle, as well as the new machine gun, fired a shorter cartridge and was deemed more accurate at long ranges. The M14 turned out to be a fluke for most of the combat units, soon replaced by the even lighter M16, which fired an even smaller cartridge that was considered a better fit for the closer-range fighting in Vietnam's jungles only months away.

As a gun enthusiast this unexpected development provided enough fascination to help me ease back to an emotional equilibrium disrupted over the previous two months by the sausage-making process of turning a flunked-out introverted college kid into the "lean mean fighting machine" promised in recruitment posters. It was the time-tested process involving colorfully worded reprimands, such as "you fucking candy asses," and strenuous physicality including many pushups, pullups and sit-ups and many many miles of running and walking, the latter while toting upwards of 100 pounds of equipment, including a rifle and a solid steel "pot," which is what we called the heavy helmets that were not designed for pencil necks.

That was over now. We'd survived. We were strong, we could shoot, club a stuffed dummy in the head with a rifle butt and stab it with a bayonet, pitch a tent, scale walls with our bare hands and swing on a rope over water. The only part of our training that remained would be a taste of what real armed combat might be like, a bloody taste in which a man could be torn to pieces by a swarm of machine gun bullets.

Our platoon of about three dozen privates rode down to the infiltration course in the back of a couple of deuce and a halfs, which is what we called the two-and-a-half-ton trucks with canvas canopies over the beds that look like olive-drab motorized Conestoga wagons. No marching today. We'd already proven ourselves on the five- and ten-mile jaunts loaded down with rifle, steel pot and gear. The trucks' squeaky brakes squeaked to a stop and somebody ordered us out. Sgt. Loudon and our lieutenant came along to watch, but once we arrived control shifted to the team that ran the course. These non-commissioned officers were lower keyed than the guys who had broken us down over eight weeks and built us into nearly men – which we were promised we would become if we survived the NIC without melting into a sobbing puddle next to a foxhole belching fiery blasts or snagged halfway under one of the barely visible strings of barbed wire stretching across our paths in several places. Or shot.

Our paths extended the length of a football field across a bed of hard-packed sand embedded with small jagged rocks. We arrived in daylight so the course staff could explain the process and guide us through a dry run to familiarize us with the drill, help prepare us mentally for the real event after nightfall.

The dry run is when I had my come to Jesus moment. We were lined up alphabetically in a trench at one end of the course facing the barrel of the Browning Machine Gun. The gun was mounted on a tripod. We'd seen it during the quick walk-through orientation at our arrival. The yard-long canister shielding its barrel contained water to keep the barrel from overheating during rapid firing. About the diameter of a quart can of tomato sauce, the canister made the barrel appear huge. It seemed aimed directly at each of us even from 100 yards away.

Pullman was on one side of me, Peary on the other. I liked Pullman, a big, quiet, good-humored fellow. Not so much Peary, who was fussier with his personal space in the barracks than needed be and carried himself with a vague air of diffident superiority. I'd have preferred a Pullman on both sides of me, but we had what we had, and Peary was my wing man on the right. For some reason I still cannot fathom I became almost paralyzed with fear in the trench awaiting the starting whistle to send us up and out and crawling down the range. When the whistle shrilled I felt too weak and shaky to make it over the lip of the trench. I watched Pullman lift himself out and then Peary started, too. Goaded by a fear even greater than the nondescript dread that was debilitating me, a fear that Peary would succeed and leave me cringing behind in the earthen womb to a fate of unthinkable shame, and hearing hoarse shouts of "Git yore goddam candy asses outta that goddam trench!" seemingly just overhead and behind me, I frantically lunged upward and dug my elbows into the shelf above me and kicked a leg up and over and pulled myself out and unto the hard rocky surface where all I saw were black boots and olive-drab butts kicking and wriggling and inching forward. Blood was pounding in my head and I fought back a nausea I knew all too well would have disgraced me as much as anything else that afternoon had I yielded to it.

Wriggling now myself and scraping over the rocks not noticing the harm they were doing me, inching toward a distant goal that had become a mirage, unreachable and taunting, is when I first began having second thoughts about why the hell I'd joined the Army. What was I doing here? I'd thrice flunked out of college and had lost my draft deferment, I'd thought that by enlisting I'd punish my dad, a lawyer, for trying to use leverage with the draft board to keep me out until I could get into a junior college, I'd enlisted for four years in the hope I'd get assigned to language school, which I figured would be the only way a dummy like me could ever learn a foreign tongue, I wanted to get the hell out of Dodge and do something completely different, maybe even see some of the world. The idea of going to war was remote. Yet, I wasn't afraid to face combat should it come to be forced upon me, or so I thought.

I was re-thinking this as I inched along toward the first strand of barbed wire I'd have to crawl under while gripping my rifle, water canteen and bayonet clanking at my side. By no means the least bit sophisticated in philosophy or political ideology, my thoughts of fighting in a war were shaped by my reading of Hemingway, Mailer and Jones, the challenges of facing danger and death, the dynamics of duty and courage. My challenge at the moment was to man-up enough to squirm under a string of barbed wire a foot off the ground without damaging my rifle or disgracing myself with anything less than a minimum of grace under pressure. But I was rethinking my capabilities, measuring them against my literatured priorities and seriously wondering whether I had what it took to become what I thought I wanted to be. I would hit the wall, it occurred to me, when the machine gun started firing and the crawl was for real.

Again it was Peary who led the way, grunting and struggling halfway under the wire just as I was about to slither under it myself to either existential glory or unimaginable dishonor. Somehow I managed to get under the damned thing without tearing shirt, pants or skin and without plugging my rifle barrel with sand. It didn't hurt my effort to hear the continual encouraging voice shouting at my candy ass to get the hell going. I forgot about Peary at that point and scrabbled along the course and crawling under a couple more strings of barbed wire, pausing to catch my breath only until the voice prompted my candy ass to get back in the game, until I made it to the concrete apron that supported the course cadre and, of course, the as-yet silent machine gun.

I was one of the last ones in and I was so exhausted I started seriously trying to think how I could escape, find a place to hide when the sun went down and the real NIC would take place.

When night fell, I was still with my platoon. I couldn't hide, I knew, because I couldn't shame myself by asking Pullman to shout "here" when my name was called, especially not trusting Peary wouldn't rat me out. The idea of facing Peary's smirk even if he didn't was more than I could abide. So I was in the trench between them when the lights came on and the whistle shrieked and the pink tracers started popping over our heads. Every fifth machine gun round was backed with phosphorous that burned throughout the bullet's trajectory. It gave the gunner an idea where his shots were going in the dark. It let us know the exercise was as real as we'd been told. The popping was from the bullets breaking the sound barrier as they passed over us. It was here that everything changed, for me.

I've worked this over in my mind many times in the fifty years since that night, and I still can't say for sure what happened. I can tell you what I remember, and that is that when I saw the tracers streaking overhead I knew somehow that all the crap we'd been told about being torn in two by bullets was just that. Crap. Those bullets were being fired so high I could have stood on a ladder and waved my arms above my head and not come anywhere near being even nicked. It never occurred to me my depth perception might have been off, that the bullets really were dangerously low and the height I perceived merely illusory. I was convinced so completely that the anxiety that had almost crippled me several hours earlier fell away and left me

87

feeling first calm and relieved and then almost giddy with excitement. I was onto something and I was going to have fun. I was up and out of that trench like a jackrabbit in a cornfield. I did the low-crawl as instructed, for a bit, but soon realized I had absolutely nothing to fear and was up on hands and knees and dashing ahead of Pullman and Peary and, in fact, most of my platoon. The TNT charges belching fire and powerful blasts out of the several mounds that jutted out of the sand around us along the course were my only distraction. But I likened them to the voices that had egged us on during the dry run. Annoying but harmless. I considered stepping over the barbed wire, but I didn't wish to become too conspicuous, as it appeared most of my platoon mates were still buying the bullshit about keeping low and safe. I was one of the first two or three to reach the concrete apron, and had the pleasure then of watching the gunner direct his fire over the course. From this perspective my conclusion was confirmed he was firing high. High was definitely the word for the moment.

Wild Card
(fiction)

Within seconds after he let up on the gas, Wendell Prine felt the kick against his back. He was not surprised that it happened, but the jolt still startled him. He didn't bother to check in his rear-view mirror, because he knew it was the white pickup that had just rammed him. Instead, he tightened his grip on the steering wheel and perched his right foot on the clutch pedal, keeping his attention on the approaching side road. At the last second he stomped the clutch to the floor and jammed the transmission into low gear. The engine howled, but the truck's forward momentum slowed as Prine tapped his brake pedal and put his truck into a sliding turn.

He waited until the truck stopped rocking on its fatigued suspension before he looked in the mirror. The white truck was there. Again, no surprise. But again, his gut clenched. Why was this happening? It was a question that had haunted him since the white truck first appeared a couple of weeks ago, and Prine was no closer to an answer.

But now he was less concerned about an answer. He was more interested in bringing an end to the torment. For this he had a plan. Until just now, when the white truck nudged his rear bumper, the plan had been mostly theory. The bump changed things.

Prine glanced at the loaded .45 pistol beside him on the seat.

Bringing it out moments earlier from its hiding place behind his feet, feeling the pistol's cold heft in his hand, had steadied him at a time when the rising adrenalin in his blood was pushing toward the twin peaks of rage and panic. He'd been uneasy borrowing the gun from his father without asking, but he knew he couldn't have explained to him why he wanted it. He'd been unable to tell anyone what was happening - not his friends, not his boss, not even his wife. He'd thought more than once about trying to tell her.

"Babe," he imagined himself saying, "there's some white dudes in a pickup truck been following me."

"Say what?" she'd have said. "Some men following you? Ooowee. Dell, you been shaking that cute ass in the wrong place again?" He'd have had the choice then of either insisting she take him seriously, and scaring hell out of her, or letting her good humor infect him and laughing it off.

Whenever his thinking reached this juncture, he opted reflexively for stoicism. As of now, it was bothering only him, he figured. If it was anything to worry about, he'd handle it. If it wasn't, or if he couldn't, well, then no sense dragging anybody else into it. He didn't feel like thinking it through any further than that. The effort just to reach that point, thinking it through to the line beyond which he'd have to start considering someone else's dignity or safety, used up as much energy as a day on the job. And it always came back to the one simple question. Why?

The first time he'd noticed the white truck it took him awhile before he felt certain its following him wasn't happenstance. It took the nearly twenty-six miles from his job site to his home, which involved eleven turns, to know for sure. As a precaution, he'd continued past his house, and when the other truck stayed on his tail he led it on a pursuit of random turns and last-second exits until eventually it dropped out. By then his heart was pounding. It pounded long after he assured himself the white truck was gone. A primitive alarm had awakened in him the instant he knew beyond any doubt that the driver of the white truck was deliberately following him.

After losing the white truck the first time, Prine pulled into his driveway and sat behind the wheel to compose himself before going inside to his family. Emotions he hadn't felt since he was a kid on a school playground - fright, mixed with an odd sense of guilt that he'd done something improper to provoke what was happening - were vying for control.

A queer intimacy had connected him with whoever was in the white truck mocking his dignity. What the hell had he done? He hadn't pulled in front of the other truck or cut it off in traffic. Had he?

Whoever was behind him had singled him out for some reason. Surely it wasn't simply racial. Things were subtler these days. Prine hadn't heard anyone call him a racial slur since high school. Nor did he go out of his way to make race an issue with people. He got along with whites, felt comfortable with most of them. If this was a racial thing, he figured, it has to be some really ignorant or sick son of a bitch, somebody off the ordinary scale. People like that existed, he knew, and the thought sent tremors of dread, alternating with flashing anger, through his bowels.

The intrusion, after permeating his nervous system with its ambivalence, bled into the ambience of his truck's cab. The little pillow he'd gorilla-glued to the console, for his elbow, the collapsible litter basket under the dash, the shabby face of the dash, the odor - an acrid mix of chemicals and eroding metal, dried mud and old upholstery - embarrassed Prine now with their sentimental frailty.

A scrap of lyric from a Doors song by Jim Morrison wormed its way into Prine's thoughts as he tried to reason his way through the implications:

There's a killer on the road,
His brain is squirming like a toad...

Prine had never really felt the lyric's malignancy until now. Emptied of its comic energy it kindled a different kind of mirth, rich with irony, which enabled him to reach an equipoise between the poles of his emotions. He sat in the truck in his driveway until the squirming of his own mind stilled and his breathing had settled into its regular rhythm, then went into his house and pretended all was well.

When it happened again three days later, then again after nearly a week, he seriously pondered whether he might be losing his mind. He still opted to keep it to himself. He couldn't go to the police. What would he tell them? He hadn't seen the truck's tag number. Hadn't even seen any faces. All he knew, from what he had glimpsed in his mirror, was that one of the occupants, the driver, wore a cap, while the other seemed to have bushy hair and maybe a beard. He assumed both were men, and he presumed they were white.

This was the fourth time. This time the truck pulled up closer behind Prine than it had previously. His heart leaped from the surge of adrenalin this provoked, making him gasp a couple of times for extra oxygen. He knew he was near to losing control. Then he remembered his father's gun. Resolve began to gather as he reached under the seat and placed his hand around the heavy piece of steel. He pulled it out and set it on the seat beside him. This action alone seemed to affirm a strategy that was born full-blown almost simultaneously, as if it had been incubating quietly at some sub level of consciousness awaiting just the right cue to emerge.

Recognition that a line had been crossed gave Prine a sudden clarity that would have been exhilarating under different circumstances. Now, however, understanding in yet another part of his brain the incongruity of what he was doing with everything that he had been up to then and understanding also that what was happening now could redefine all that had come before and drastically alter or conclude what might remain for him, a grim deliberateness took over. Then came the bump, which sealed his fate.

The crossroad Prine had turned onto led into a heavily wooded area broken only by occasional small farms and trailer homes. Winter had stripped most of the leaves from the maples, gums and oaks, creating a limbed webbing around the blots of cedar and scrub pine. Prine's mind was racing now, but everything else seemed to have slowed or stopped, separated into surreal increments.

He hadn't gotten a clear view yet of his tormentors, but his imagining how they looked fed his determination to end the terror they were bringing to him: grinning cruelly, stupidly. Yes, he could shoot them. Damned right he could. God damn them to hell. He hadn't bothered them. They had no God damned right to bother him. The God damned bastards…

He looked for a place to pull off the road for a confrontation. Before he could find one, the white pickup started to pass. Prine could see the passenger window rolling down as the truck drew abreast. He reached for his pistol. Then he saw a flash of something in the other truck's window. A gold badge in a leather folder. Shit. The bushy-haired man holding the badge motioned Prine to pull off the road. Prine did. He rolled down his window as the cop got out of the other truck. Prine stashed the pistol back under his seat, pulled his wallet out of his back pocket and had his operator's license and registration in hand by the time the cop, wearing dirty jeans and a faded red plaid shirt, walked up, his breath steaming in the December chill.

The cop was wearing the kind of mirrored sunglasses cops universally seemed to favor. He barely glanced at Prine's documents before speaking.

"Get out, nigger."

"Excuse me, officer, what have I done?" said Prine, trying to sound calm, while his brain worked frantically. He felt a giddiness lighten his head as he stared at the double blip that was him in the cop's reflecting lenses.

"I said get out of the truck, nigger," the cop snarled, this time jerking his arm back as if reaching for the gun on his hip. Prine was astounded when the cop's hand came up and stuck a gun through the window. The gun had a huge barrel, which, when his eyes focused on the small hole in its end, Prine realized was a silencer. He experienced an odd detachment as his prostate relaxed and warm urine gushed over his thighs. His spirit froze with the sudden understanding of exactly what was happening and what it was that he had to do, and that he was going to try to do it. Still staring at the grotesque muzzle inches from his face, he rocked forward to grab the gun under his seat, raising his left hand to smack the intruding barrel away. He watched it follow his head. Then, as the fingers of his right hand found the grip of his own pistol and the back of his left hand barely touched the other, he saw a flash of light stab out from the little hole in the center of the massive barrel. He heard nothing. Felt nothing, except a momentary intense itch in his left eye.

The man standing outside Prine's truck squeezed the trigger three more times, feeling the pistol jump slightly in his hand as it coughed the .22-caliber hollowpoint slugs into Prine's brain. The body jerked upright and sideways across the seat, then flopped half a dozen times like a landed fish, shoes scraping under the dashboard while the bowels evacuated loudly, sending their stench to overpower the nip of hot gasses from the fired cartridges.

Prine's executioner waited until the legs and splayed arms ceased their final, shuddering spasms and the body at last was still. Then he opened the truck's door and knelt beside the body, peering inside the cab until he found the victim's wallet. He took the money and replaced the license and vehicle registration, then tossed the wallet on the ground. He ripped a gold chain from the dead man's neck, and climbed into the white pickup, which slung gravel against Prine's truck as it spun through a U-turn and headed back to the main road.

Achtung!

Hüte dich vor dem Elefanten!

Um, sorry 'bout that. Flashbacks can be horrible. I believe the above is German for "beware the elephant!" or something along that line.

This might even be what the old man shouted at us as he clicked back the hammer of his drilling and swung its three barrels past our torsos to emphasize his momentary absolute superiority. Too heavy to hold horizontally for long, though, he rested the butt of his massive weapon on one of his leather-clad feet after making certain we understood where we stood, so to speak.

Fortunately for all three of us, Ralph spoke pretty good German, and he and the old man carried on an uneven conversation for awhile - uneven in that it came in spurts of spittle-spraying earnestness and vehemence, interspersed with hesitations, hand gestures and halting efforts to clarify this or that nuance, which evidently had not been clarified for one or the other.

Ralph and I had gotten into this predicament while trying to re-enter our post near the West German village of Rothwesten. It was a small post that had served the Luftwaffe during WWII as an airfield, camouflaged to resemble a small resort or exclusive school campus. The buildings were of a Swiss chalet design, and the airplanes - Messerschmitts, we believed - were housed beneath a sheep-grazing pasture, to emerge for flight exercises up a ramp and out a trap door.

The field itself consisted of a wire mesh through which grass could grow for the sheep to eat, theoretically fooling Allied surveillance from above to not suspect that this quaint pastoral setting concealed mighty warplanes bent on wiping democracy from the face of the Earth. *Jawohl!*

Whether or not it fooled anybody from the air, eventually troops under the command of Gen. George S. Patton, according to the legend we were taught, found the place and were rolling through the front gate as the beaten Nazis skedaddled out the rear.

It was this rear gate that Ralph and I were planning to enter after a walk through wood and field, over hill and dale to Rothwesten for a bowl of oxtail soup, a locally brewed beer or two and some mild flirtation with indigenous fraulein possibilities.

As dusk settled over the countryside, we trod back to our post thru wood and field and over hill and dale, sated gastronomically, a tad tipsy and our egos mildly flattered and hopeful, and decided to hell with walking all the way around the post to enter the guarded front gate, where we might have gotten written up for one thing or another.

It was as we approached the barely visible, unguarded, swinging gate in the fence that a shadowy figure popped out from behind some shrubbery and confronted us with the uniquely German long arm that usually consists of a shotgun barrel affixed to a couple of rifle barrels - one large caliber and one small. At that moment, at that range, even at that time of dying day, our kraut-chewing interloper could have taken both of us down, shooting from the hip, with both eyes closed, while screaming maniacally, "Veddddy eenterestink, but dumb!"

I imagined him as one of the Nazis who'd fled Patton, who'd never surrendered, who lived in a nearby cave awaiting just this moment to assert the last bitter gasp of his Fuhrer's furious Reich. *Achtungaufweidenhoserschplatzerkeugelheffenpfeiperplunk!* Perhaps.

This grotesquely armed apparition was decked out in the ubiquitous lederhosen (with suspenders), a waist-length jacket, wool knee socks, clodhoppers on his feet and a felt hat that sprouted what presumably had been the most glorious tail feather of a large bird of prey.

Whatever Ralph was thinking, he kept his emotions largely in check, reasoning with Fritz in Fritz's own tongue, pretty much, and ultimately succeeded in persuading this rear guard Herr Somethingorother to carefully lower the hammer of his triple threat boomer and correspondingly soften his voice to approximate a more civil approach to his NATO ally.

He watched while we slipped through the gate and fled with measured, though brisk dignity into the sanctuary of our Army brethren.

Ralph waited until we were out of earshot, in the event that Herman could speak excellent English and was waiting for some smartass remark to propel his thumb backward on the hammer once again, to give me the lowdown.

It seems that Schultz was a minor government official, the equivalent of a game warden, who had merely suspected us of poaching. Most likely he would have let us off the hook, regardless of Ralph's impassioned defensive chattering, once he realized we were unarmed and unburdened by any ill-gotten game.

Had I known this then and possessed the presence of mind, I wish I'd asked Ralph to ask Adolf if I could rent his artillery for a moment to hurl some ballistics at a large tree.

As it is, I have yet to fire a single drilling barrel, and most likely will never be able to afford to do so.

Manhattan Mayhap

It was not wise to shout a Russian greeting at a motorcade carrying a Soviet premier in 1967. I could have been arrested or even shot. That I wasn't, turned out to be the second Mr. Magoo moment of my brief visit to New York.

The first had been moments earlier when one of the young men in the group I walked past coming up the stairs of a subway exit approached me too closely and asked for a light. "Sorry, I don't smoke," I said honestly, shrugging and offering a friendly smile. I had never stopped walking, and I continued up the cement stairs. Nothing more was said. I learned much later that I likely had been the target of a street gang's classic set up. Had I stopped and lit the man's cigarette I might have been robbed, or worse.

It was midday in mid-June 1967. I was wearing my Army uniform, having just returned from West Germany after serving a three-year tour. Perhaps it was the uniform or the sense of purpose in my carriage that allowed me passage from the gang's predatory intent. Perhaps there were too many other potential targets or witnesses around, or maybe it just wasn't my time.

I had arrived by bus from Fort Dix, New Jersey, where I'd mustered out. I had several hours to kill before my train left to take me home. It was my first time in New York. I'd left my bags in a locker at the train station and was doing a walkabout to see as much as I could before catching the train.

This was 43 years ago, folks, so my memory is serving up only the most indelible images. I assume I had a quick lunch, probably after buying my train ticket. I remember carrying a tube of toothpaste and a tooth brush in a paper bag, which I must have purchased about the same time. I was holding the bag when I reached Fifth Avenue at Rockefeller Plaza. It struck me as odd that there was no traffic on the avenue. None. But there were police officers, some on horseback, positioned along both sides as far as I could see in either direction. It seemed I was the only civilian present, but none of the officers acknowledged or approached me.

After a minute or so just standing there wondering what was up, I saw movement to my left. Several motorcycles ahead of a black car aflutter with flags were rolling up the avenue. As they neared, I saw others following closely. It was a motorcade for somebody important. I remembered seeing headlines on the newspaper that morning declaring that Soviet Premier Alexei Kosygin was in the city to speak at the United Nations. The Six-Day War between Israel and its neighbors had been fought about two weeks earlier and the Soviets had called for an emergency U.N. General Assembly session to discuss Middle East security.
My papers for an early release from active duty to return to college had come through while my unit was packed and awaiting in a row of vehicles for orders to be flown to Wheelus Air Base in Tripoli, Libya. Our mission was to have evacuated U.S. citizens in case the war expanded to that country. My emotions were mixed - excitement to be going home tempered by disappointment that I was leaving my unit in a time of crisis. As things turned out, my buddies never left Germany. The war ended shortly after my flight touched down at Fort Dix.

On Fifth Avenue now, my sense of its importance grew exponentially as the motorcade drew nearer. This was coincidence of historic proportion for me, something to tell my grandchildren, my dad would have said. Nearly four years earlier I'd been in an airplane en route from Fort Jackson, South Carolina, South Carolina, to Fort Devens, Massachusetts, when JFK was murdered. Learned about the shooting when our plane stopped in Philadelphia to refuel. Learned the president was dead when the driver pulled our bus to the curb in Worcester, Mass., so we could buy EXTRA editions of the local newspaper from a kid on a corner. Official motorcades have sparked an ambivalence in me ever since.

Small American flags sprouted from the fenders of the first couple of cars. Men in business suits walked briskly alongside, their heads swiveling constantly. Then more motorcycles, ridden by helmeted police officers, and then...another black limousine, accompanied by more walking men in suits. A scowling man leaned out of the front passenger window and two other suited men stood on a platform at the limo's rear. Red flags fluttered on this one's fenders. This was Kosygin.

"*Zdrastvutya!*" I shouted triumphantly at the car. I'd studied Russian in the Army. I was being a good American welcoming a visitor to my country with a greeting in his own language. I was being stupid.

Before I could take a breath to shout a followup "*Prevetstvovatye!*" (welcome) the man leaning out of the car leaned even further and fixed me with an ungracious glare. Simultaneously, the man on my side of the limo's rear platform turned to me, as well. I don't remember if he glared or not. I most likely didn't notice, as my eyes were fixed on the submachine gun in his hands, its lethal barrel pointed straight at my grinning idiot face.

The grin vanished as I suddenly remembered the paper bag in my hand. I dropped it at my feet and spread my arms wide, empty palms facing front. I awaited the *ratatatat* from the rear of Kosygin's limo that would assure my footnote in history with no grandchildren to read about it. The motorcade eased on by. It seemed every visible face in and around the motorcade vehicles glared at me until they were out of sight. I don't remember if the New York police officers were aware of what had just happened. None of them approached me then or after the parade had passed.

I imagine it wasn't too much longer before I started breathing again, picked up my paper bag and sauntered back from whence I came.

What If?
(fiction)

Static electricity danced in the air a full half minute after the others left, closing the door behind them. I remained seated in the padded chair I usually occupied in front of the historic desk. I had begun to rise with the others, but the Boss caught my eye and jerked his head slightly toward the private office adjoining the one he used for ceremonies and informal staff meetings. I sat back down, still stunned by the intensity of the meeting and glad to see the Boss was making no effort to rise from behind the desk, but had leaned back into his chair from the elbows-planted-on-desk position he ordinarily favored. We stared at each other.

"What the fuck is the matter with you, sir? You're throwing this presidency, *your* presidency out the goddam window! Worse than that, you're letting down – fuck with the euphemisms – you're betraying, you're fucking the people who elected you. They trusted that you would be better than the asshole running against you. They trusted you goddammit when you said things would change. The people who elected you trusted you, you goddam chickenshit asshole! And you're too god damned chickenshit to do right by them. Fuck you, sir. I quit this goddam fucking chickenshit job!" Eugene O'Malley was sobbing, close to hysteria, when he finished this rant, shouting louder and louder until his voice broke into a falsetto on the last "chickenshit" and mangling the "job" to a grunt.

The Boss said nothing. He seemed to have turned into the kind of wax figure that belonged in Madame Tussaud's. Shocking as O'Malley's outburst was, it came as less a surprise than had it been one of the others in the room. O'Malley, a former trial lawyer and the Boss's brilliant but mercurial political advisor, was not shy about using profanity and raising his voice. The real surprise was his addressing the Boss as "sir" during the diatribe. He had never been that formal in my experience and we both went back with the Boss all the way to his first campaign for a House seat from Virginia's First District. Another thing different this time was that O'Malley had never gotten quite this worked up. He had threatened numerous times to quit, but this was the first time he'd actually said "I quit" and stormed out of the room. Also, he had never used the word "asshole" in the presence of Vice President Schwammel. Perhaps it encouraged him that she was almost as angry as he over the Boss's apparent paralysis in the face of fairly mild congressional resistance to his tax proposal.

"You're becoming a laughing stock," Schwammel said in her husky, country club voice. "The cartoonists are shrinking you more and more each Sunday. Remember Jimmy Carter? He was about the size of an ant by the time he got the boot. You're not much bigger than one now. The Post and the Times are both ridiculing you. You read the papers, Bubby. They're passing right over you now. They're dissing the office, for Christ's sake."

The Boss's face, with his prominent eyebrows pushing wrinkles into his expansive forehead, had conveyed a weary good humor at the start of the morning meeting. He could hold that demeanor indefinitely and he did so for most of the hour. But now, responding to Schwammel, the skin around his eyes seemed to crinkle in a way that suggested pain, giving the eyes a haunted look that also suggested the desperation of a cornered animal.

"Adele," he said, his voice lower and slower than usual as he enunciated his words with a deliberate precision that signaled he was losing patience, "I'm going to say this one more time and then, that's it. OK? I'm not here to please the Post or the Times or the cartoonists. I know they reflect and even influence public opinion, but they are not sitting in this chair, although, Frankly, there are days when it might be fun to trade jobs with Paul Kruggerand. But only for a day. I'd hate to see his blood pressure charts if he sat in this chair for more than one day."

Ordinarily a line like this broke the tension in a contentious meeting. Relieved laughter was the reward. Not this time. After a couple of silent beats, Schwammel continued, "Frankly, Boss, I'm worried. This is an unnecessary political imbroglio. You could have called their bluff a month ago. Your reasoning at the time was, well, reasonable, but that was assuming they would blink first. They haven't, and now it's almost too late. We're too close to the brink. Out of options. You must take executive action. We have no choice."

"Adele," he started, but this is when Gene cut in. The Boss sat rigidly but poker-faced during the diatribe. After Gene stormed out, the Boss made a show of checking his watch and then dismissed the rest with a terse, "That's it for now. Don't worry. Gene's got a lot on his mind. He'll be OK."

The private office is much smaller and more utilitarian, with books piled on the floor and papers strewn across the plastic folding Lowe's table he used as a desk. A traditional wooden desk with drawers against one wall held a computer and more books. He motioned me to the comfortable stuffed couch against the opposite wall. It was where he slept occasionally after a long night of work with only a couple of hours before the next work day would begin. He waited until I was seated before rolling the padded chair from behind the table over next to the couch and lowering himself into its cushions.

In one hand he held a remote, with which he activated a projection screen that unfurled from the ceiling above the other desk. He then pointed the device at a projection box on the table and lit up the screen, all the while not saying a word. Within seconds we were watching the most horrifying video I had ever seen and hope I never see the likes of again. It was obviously an old video, as the colors were faded and there were sporadic distracting flashes of white, indicating scratches and the other signs of deterioration incurred by film over time.

The scene was of a sparse grove of trees at the end of an expanse of untended grass. The camera that recorded this scene slowly moved toward the trees until I could see they were atop a hill overlooking a city street. There was activity in the street, but it was out of focus as the camera had fixed on the figures of two men between two of the trees. Both men were dressed in dark clothing. One was leaning against a wooden fence, his back to the camera, and the other was standing beside him peering through a telescope that was mounted on a tripod. Both men were looking down at the street.

I started feeling a little dizzy watching this, as something terribly familiar was emerging from my memory and mingling with the images on the screen. Before I knew for sure what I was seeing, the man leaning against the fence jerked suddenly and a puff of smoke rose from in front of him. He jerked again, releasing a second puff of smoke. After a couple of seconds both men gathered their equipment and turned toward the camera. This is when I first recognized that the man who had been leaning against the fence was holding a rifle. At about the same time two shadows emerged from either side of the men. The shadows came into focus and I could see they were also dressed in dark clothing. Both were holding pistols with bulging barrels. The guns jerked and the other two men, the one with the rifle and the one with the telescope, staggered and fell to the ground. Then two more figures appeared with what appeared to be body bags. The four standing figures lifted the two men I now assumed were dead into the body bags, zipped them up and carried them away from the camera. The video ended at this point.

"Holy fuck!" I blurted when the Boss turned to me. "What the fuck?" I said, feeling stupid, stunned and scared out of my wits. I was nauseous.

"Holy fuck, indeed," murmured the Boss.

"Where did this come from?"

"It was in the mail. Last month With the newspapers."

"No shit?"

"No shit."

"Why didn't you say something?"

"What good would that have done?"

"Well, did you tell Rufus?" Rufus Johnstone was agent-in-charge of the White House security detail.

"I didn't know who I could trust, Al. It's that simple."

"Me? You couldn't trust me? What the hell, why are you trusting me now?"

"I don't care anymore. Whoever delivered it either didn't know what it was or they had him or her by the short hairs. Whoever sent this has this presidency by the short hairs, has probably had every presidency by the short hairs since then and probably always will."

"Yeah, but..."

"Yeah."

Mettle Test

 Traditionally the projectile that bursts from the barrels of firearms and screams toward its target at supersonic speeds is composed largely of lead. In some configurations the lead projectile is sheathed in another, harder metal, such as copper or brass, to enable better penetration into its target.

Lead is a heavy, poisonous metal, a neurotoxin that accumulates in soft tissue and bone, which is why we spent about $800 having paint scrapings in our old house tested for lead when our daughter was born. Despite the expense, we sighed heavily with relief when the tests came back negative. Nonetheless, we cautioned her through the toddler years not to chip off paint flakes to eat, advice I'm pretty sure she took despite the danger that such warnings often increase children's curiosity to try the forbidden anti-fruits. To my knowledge she never tried to lick a flagpole in freezing weather, either.

Let us segue now to the story prompted by our interest in the dangers of lead. In this scenario we're back to the problems of its more immediate penetration into soft tissue and bone.

Smacking of the classic feud between Elmer Fudd and Bugs Bunny, the "wascally wabbit," Kenny and I, then, were the wabbits - 12 or 13 or so years of age - and a neighbor of Kenny's, whose name has vanished into the deep subconscious, was Mr. Fudd.

Kenny and I were goofing along the banks of the Elba River, which runs through our town in Wisconsin and past the house where Kenny lived then. Its dam powered our generating plant at the time. The river also contained reliable holes for catching small catfish we called bullheads, and, when the water level was low, a kid could fill pails with clams stranded in its muddy bed.

On this day, the clams had no need to fear our presence, as we were more interested in the lure of blackberries that grew along

the bank. Our only problem was that the legal distinction between riparian rights of landowners along the river, which did not include the hapless clams, did, however protect any flora that might extend up from the water to the adjoining property. In this case, the blackberries we coveted belonged to Mr. Fudd.

And on this day we ventured nearer Mr. Fudd's property than usual for the very purpose of sampling his luscious fruit, which flourished along the stretch of land between the river and the nearby road. Kenny had cautioned me that Mr. Fudd, who seemed always to be at home, wasn't especially liberal about folks messing in his blackberry patch.

We hadn't eaten more than a handful of the succulent tangy black morsels when, indeed, Kenny's cautionary note was confirmed by the appearance in denim overalls and straw hat of the dreaded Mr. Fudd. What really got our attention, though, was the long-barreled gun he was holding.

"Run," ordered Kenny. We ran, scratching our thighs and arms on the briars that blackberry bushes brandish as a first line of defense against poachers such as we. Mr. Fudd was the second line.

"Boom," we heard from behind us, a sound, which, until that moment, because of the intent we knew was behind it, produced an effect unlike any other I had experienced in my short life. We ran harder.

"Boom!" This time Kenny yelled, "Ouch!" I was too dumbfounded to yell, but I felt a stinging sensation across my back, just below the shoulder blades. We ran, stumbling, giggling, spitting berry juice onto the foliage around us, until we made it to safety behind the flowing branches of the willow tree that hid us from Fudd, which was as good at this point as if it had provided serious ballistic cover.

I told Kenny that I had been hit. My back still stung, but not as badly as I'd thought it would with a mortal wound. Nor did I feel the inevitable hot liquid streaming down my back as it likely would were I bleeding to death on the Elba River bank this lazy, crazy summer afternoon.

I felt Kenny's hand on my back, scraping. He held it out in front of me. Little white chips lay nestled in his palm.

"Salt," he said. "He's shooting rock salt."

We peered into each other's eyes, then back at the small chunks of salt in Kenny's hand. I checked his back. As he wasn't wearing a shirt, there was no forensic evidence of the shooting in sight. There was blood streaming down his arms, but this came from the blackberry briar scratches. On his back I found only red blotches, where presumably the same projectiles that had lodged in my T-shirt had blasted his skin.

After a moment or two we cautiously peeked out through the willow branches to see Fudd still standing in his blackberry patch, holding the shotgun in both hands and staring hard in our direction.

"YOU'LL BE SORRY WHEN MY DAD GETS HOME!" Kenny yelled at him. "HE'LL CALL THE POLICE, AND THEY'LL ARREST YOU!"

That would never happen, of course. Kenny knew full well that he stood to get some far more serious blotches across his back if his dad ever learned of our adventure.

Old Fudd yelled something back at us. We didn't hear clearly what he said, but no doubt it was something along the lines of what the police would do to us when he, Fudd, told them we'd been trespassing. We suspected he was bluffing, too.

We didn't tell our parents.

To this day - until now - the matter has remained a secret between Kenny and me, and, of course, Mr. Fudd.

Turnings
(fiction)

"Help me," the man said in his mind. He lay beside the folding camp stool alone in the middle of the woods, in the clearing where he and the dog always rested. It was the halfway point of their daily walk, about a mile up the trail from the edge of the woods that abutted the property where they lived. The winding trail had been cleared by their neighbor, who owned the woods and otherwise left it undisturbed. It was late spring, and tendrils of new blackberry bushes and other green growth were pushing up, making it harder to walk along the ruts and stumps and sun-bleached disintegrating tree parts that littered the way.

The man was alone because the dog had known something was wrong and had broken off and headed back soon after they started. She had acted a little strangely herself, and the man had shown his impatience, which quickly dispirited her. She usually burst up the trail, sniffing insatiably at anything that caught her eye. Occasionally she'd double back to him or follow her nose off the trail into the underbrush, and sometimes the man had to call her to keep her from straying too far or from finding something rotting to roll in.

She lived for these walks. She'd doze morosely in her bed by the fireplace until she sensed the man getting ready each day. Her excitement when he finally appeared in his walking clothes, carrying his aluminum stick and wearing his backpack and blaze orange hat, inspired her to dance, her toenails clacking on the hardwood floor. Sometimes she'd whine and squeal and even bark with unbearable anticipation. At the front door, when he put on his mud boots, he'd let her outside to relieve some of her tension. And if it took a moment or two longer than usual to change from his moccasins to the boots, or to get something he'd forgotten for the walk, she would attack him playfully when he finally emerged on the porch.

"No no!" he would have to order her firmly, raising a hand to keep her from jumping on him. She always obeyed. She knew he didn't like the physical contact that she loved, and she reluctantly heeded his wishes in this regard. The walk meant that much to her.

This one started out much the same for the dog, but for the man all morning a dark essence had been migrating almost imperceptibly from a corner of his heart. This gloomy patch advanced in a distinct lurch moments after the man stepped into the woods from the groomed acreage behind his house, provoked by the contrast he immediately felt with the sense of pleasant anticipation this transition brought as a rule. It wasn't the same. A pinch of impatience in the man, different from the dog's eagerness, had poisoned the moment they always enjoyed at the start of the morning trek. The dog sensed something amiss.

"C'mon! Let's go!" he said, his voice so prickly with annoyance that instead of bounding ahead she only looked up at him as if confused. He tried again, harshly now as he swung an arm up the trail, "Tasha! Let's go!" Obediently she loped ahead, but stopped after ten feet or so, forcing him to stop as well to avoid running into her. "Tasha! Let's go! Wheeeeeee! Yeeha!" he said. The fake excitement in his voice didn't fool the dog, who now stared at him, a mixture of forlorn guilt and stubbornness clouding her liquid brown eyes.

He stepped around her and headed up the trail, figuring she'd follow eventually. He looked back several times to see if she had started after him, but saw her merely sitting on the trail, eyes fixed on him, making no move to continue the walk. The man called out each time he looked back, to no avail. He even called out to her a couple of times after he'd rounded the first curve atop the hill and could no longer see her, then finally gave up when it became apparent she wasn't coming along.

The man at first took the dog's refusal to accompany him as defiance. A sour pulse of resentment welled up, and he looked for something to kick in retaliation. But the irritation had begun receding almost as soon as it appeared, replaced incrementally by a sense of relief from the vigilance walking with the dog always demanded. This affected his pace, which quickly relaxed to follow his whims, dallying at a patch of shy green tendrils that reached up from a winter's nap or pausing to study a tangle of fallen branches he'd not noticed before. He often found random shapes intriguing, especially if their proximity to one another suggested a pattern of some sort. The surprise of wildflowers always delighted him, although he seldom bothered to look at them closely.

But now, with nothing else to tug at his attention, the man stooped and inspected a spray of tiny yellow blossoms affixed to a branching purple stem several feet from the ground. The pale flowers perched in groups of about a dozen each in multiple clusters on thin green stems above collars of leaves that seemed to emerge randomly from the branches. As he drew closer, the man saw that each cluster contained seven groups of the flowers. Spellbound by their beauty, he thought to pick a sprig of the flowers. Instead, he straightened up, took a ballpoint pen and a small spiral-bound notebook from his jacket and noted the find. He jotted down what he'd seen as accurately as he could in the hope of being able to learn the plant's identity when he returned home. He felt pleased that after glancing at these little flowers on previous walks from a distance he'd finally made the effort to look at them closely. He continued up the trail, buoyed by a surge of energy that offered maybe an antidote to the gloom in his spirit that he knew loitered too near.

It was about then he caught the sour sweet odor of rot that he knew was from the buck that had died some months back, during winter, back off a side trail that he and the dog were avoiding. The man intended to wait until decomposition was complete so that Tasha would no longer be tempted to rush upon it and roll with delirious joy in the putrid mess. He had stopped her at the brink of doing just that when she'd discovered the corpse as the two were taking this detour around part of the main trail. The dog had dashed into the underbrush, bounding with the sort of excitement that only another animal -- a rabbit, most likely -- could rouse in her. Glancing ahead of her to see what she might be chasing, his eyes caught the gray mass that quickly came into focus as the deer's upper torso and heavily antlered head. It wasn't responding to Tasha, who had drawn to within about ten feet before the man could shout for her to come back. So unusually loud and harsh was his voice that Tasha instantly stopped, turned and trotted back to the trail. The man's insistence was so firm that she followed him dutifully to the main trail without once swinging her head back toward what must have struck her at the moment of discovery as El Dorado.

The man was proud of the dog's discipline, then and throughout the winter months when their walks would bring them to the side trail's juncture and Tasha at first would swing her head persuasively, tail wagging fiercely, as if to will them down the inexplicably forbidden path. On the innocent days before they'd stumbled onto the dead buck the two would play a little game when they reached this juncture.

"Should we go down this path today, or should we go straight," the man would ask, and most times the dog would eagerly lead them down the side trail. Sometimes she'd forget about it and plunge right past as if in a hurry to get home, but mostly she'd choose the diversion. Their game ended, of course, after the grotesque discovery. Tasha invariably would pick up the rotten scent long before reaching the side trail, and, although she'd be sniffing breezes with the refined attention of a Sherlock Holmes, she soon caught on that the path to rapture was no longer an option. The man liked to think it was partly dignity that eventually kept her from embarrassing both of them with a scene when the temptation beckoned.

He looked up over the trees where the corpse lay, finding it curious again that there weren't vultures, either circling overhead or lurking in the high branches. It had been so all winter, not seeing vultures near the site, which should have been a mecca for carrion feeders of all kinds. He'd seen vultures on the walks, but never near the dead buck. He mentioned this once to his neighbor, and added, "Maybe they think it's a decoy."

"Yeah, too good to be true," the neighbor had said.

Today, when the man reached the head of the side trail he considered checking out the buck just to see how far along the decomposition had come. He decided against it, in part because he still wasn't sure the dog wouldn't change her mind and come along, but more probably because his curiosity wasn't enough to prevail over the bleakness he expected to find. Thus he barely paused before continuing up the main trail.

It took him another twenty minutes to reach the far end of the trail and the clearing where he and the dog always rested. It seemed to him that he'd made better time today than usual, but after thinking about it he allowed that this impression might be a result of his simply being unfettered of having to heed the dog's distractions, her following scents into underbrush and having to be called back to the trail. He recognized, too, that without the dog on his mind he could follow his own interests and whims, and that this would naturally accelerate his sense of time.

And yet, now that he was ready to rest, he acknowledged that he did feel a bit alone as he began the rituals that came at this stage:

hanging his walking stick on the branch of a small holly tree, tugging the straps of his small backpack from his shoulders and hanging the pack on the other side of the tree on the stub of a branch he'd clipped off with his knife for that purpose, then unzipping the pack and removing the aluminum camp stool, unfolding it, planting its three legs on the ground and lowering himself to the netting seat.

Because the dog wasn't with him, he left the small plastic bowl he carried in the pack for her water, and he also left the two plastic bottles of water in their netting pockets on the sides of the pack. One of the bottles was for him, but he wasn't thirsty.

Sitting on the stool, he glanced over to where the dog usually lay, under a pin oak, eating the chlorophyll treat he always brought along for her and which now remained in his shirt pocket. He groped at the pocket and took the cellophane-wrapped, bone-shaped treat out and looked at it, and was suddenly struck by a sense of grief that amazed him. He felt as if Tasha were dead. He wanted her to come bounding up the trail into the clearing. He even called her name several times, hoping that she'd just been lagging behind. He crinkled the cellophane wrapper on the treat. That at home could bring her to him from four rooms away. She loved these treats. He called her name several more

times. Then, as suddenly as it came, the terrible sensation he felt -- almost a seizure, it seemed -- passed. Whew. He tried to celebrate with a chuckle. His abdomen lurched a couple of times, feebly, but no sound came from his throat. He managed to pull in a deep breath and release it in a pursed-lip sigh. Not yet out of the woods, he thought, and made another unsuccessful stab at a laugh, this time to acknowledge the pun.

A wave of fatigue washed over him. He decided that a drink of water would be good, and he started to rise from the stool to retrieve one of the bottles from his backpack. But the fatigue overcame this effort. He slumped on the stool. His thirst could wait.

At this point he began to sweat, and a dreadful alienation crept into his bones. It was like nothing he'd ever experienced. It started visually. Opening his eyes and seeing his jeans, he found them unfamiliar. They were his, he knew, but the cut and the fabric -- even the color -- were strange. Not at all friendly. With considerable effort he leaned back and lifted his head, which had been hanging loosely, chin against his chest. He lifted his head enough so that he could see the bushes and trees in front of him. Again, unfamiliar. Somewhat recognizable, but not comfortably so. They seemed to be staring back at him as if he were intruding, as if they didn't want him to be there. They appraised him coldly, on the verge of anger.

The sky might offer some reassurance, he hoped, and tilted back some more, rolling his eyes to see above the frightening treetops. The sky was clear and blue. He knew this should make him feel better, but it didn't. The sun was behind him. He wondered if the sun would make him feel better if he turned around and looked at it. But he knew he wouldn't be able to rise from the stool. Despite the sun and the lack of clouds, the sky intimidated him. This frightened him more than anything yet. There were no vapor trails from airplanes. There was always at least one vapor trail, usually two or three up there whenever he looked. He'd always found something reassuring about seeing evidence that other people were up there, giving the sky some dimension, some humanity. The only other time he could remember seeing the sky devoid of vapor trails was the day after the Twin Towers attack. He and a friend were in the parking lot of a pancake house, and they looked up and noted the eeriness of a sky that reflected a nation frozen in terror. The man shivered, and then he and his friend went inside and ate a hearty breakfast. That terror passed.

The man dearly hoped now that this terror, too, would pass. He searched the treetops for birds, even the vultures, as he yearned for anything alive that might deliver him. If there were birds, he couldn't see them. If they were singing or calling each other, he couldn't hear them.

Flat on the ground beside the stool, he couldn't remember how he got there. He didn't remember falling off. He might have tried to rise and simply been too weak to do so and even too feeble to sit back down on the stool, and then simply curled up in the weeds, stones and twigs next to the stool, which, when he twisted his head slightly he could see was still standing, which was an indication that he hadn't fallen, or the stool likely would have collapsed next to him.

He was now shivering and drenched in sweat, trembling actually, trembling violently. Even his legs were shaking, boots making little kicks in the dirt. Oddly, the shaking and shivering ceased when his mind came around to the thought that he might have been lying there, in the same position, for a long time. He knew that his sense of time had become skewed and that whatever he might be thinking about the duration of his predicament was probably too subjective to be reliable.

He was forgetting to breathe. He felt his sense of control over anything at all leaving him, that, if he wasn't already there, he was devolving toward complete helplessness. He took a certain comfort in knowing this, a certain "to hell with it" sense of giving in to whatever it was that was taking over. Then, at what seemed the penultimate shift to oblivion, something deep in his mind that still rebutted surrender made it's desperate plea:

"Help me."

His words were not spoken, but the words he heard next most definitely were. They were uttered by a female, whether young or old he couldn't tell. He didn't recognize the voice, yet it sounded familiar and deeply stirring. The voice, speaking gently but firmly and with a tone that carried a sublime urgency, instantly banished the darkness that was devouring him. As the three words were spoken and without any context other than the immediate, they meant nothing literally to the man. Yet, despite their inscrutability, in concert they stroked him as if a bolt from Genesis.

"We love you!"

There was an incredulity in the voice that came through as an emphasis on the word "love." As if the word "love" were where the power lay and that if he couldn't see this and hadn't known he was loved by whomever was speaking then woe be unto him if he allowed himself to slip away without a fight. And woe be unto him if he didn't get his ass up off the ground right this instant and get his shit together. We love you, dammit!

But it was something more than this. There was pain in the voice that also cried to him that his recognition and acceptance of the spoken love was vital to the speaker. We love you! Please, please believe this! A frail upturn of the word "love" touched him with a deeper, dearer plea: It breaks my heart to think that you might not know this, or that you don't care.

"Where are you?" he blurted aloud, moving his head and trying to get to his knees. His voice came stronger now: "Come here! Let me see you! Help me get up!" Nothing. No response. No more voice. He'd imagined it? Not a chance, it was as real as anything he'd ever known. Someone nearby had spoken aloud. He hoped it was to him. He knew it was to him. But why?

And who is "we," he asked himself, almost thinking who the hell is we, but biting his mental tongue in time. It didn't matter. The more who loved him at this moment the better. He burst into tears and wept. This went on seemingly for an eternity. His weeping grew in intensity until it reached hysteria, and he pounded the ground with his fists and kicked his legs, and when he finally was finished, when he'd thoroughly used up whatever reservoir of energy he'd had and he lay on his side, spent and dazed, he became aware that he had urinated in his pants, and this made him laugh. But he was too tired to offer more than a few gasps and choking coughs.

He wobbled to his feet and stood, swaying and taking deep breaths until he felt strong enough to take a step. This he did, unsteadily, but he remained upright, and then took another and then another.

The return trip down the trail seemed interminable. Weak as he was, he had to stop and rest several times along the way. After the first such break, he didn't bother to put the folding stool back in his pack, but simply carried it in the hand he didn't use for his walking stick. To his mind, the day had turned from a black and white film noir to a Disney in Technicolor. The birds were back, chattering, zipping around overhead and perched in bushes and on tree branches. Wildflowers he'd barely noticed before seemed to pop up at his feet all along the trail. Yellow blossoms of different sizes and shapes, tiny purple violets, masses of delicate bluets and one tall wine-colored lupine spike that he'd taken the trouble to identify once because it looked so unusual.

He felt as if he were striding through a gauntlet of merry well-wishers. He proceeded cautiously nonetheless, understanding that treachery could be lurking anywhere, hidden or merely waiting patiently in plain sight to be recognized. He strained to regain the sound of the voice that could be his talisman. We love you.

Oh, God, yes, thank you. Thank you.

Stepping out of the woods into his back yard brought practiced patterns quickly into focus. He saw the dog, lying on her mat on the back porch, looking his way. Slowly he walked to the porch. "Tasha," he said gently. She stared at him, not moving, her eyes tentative.

He stopped at the foot of the steps.

"I'm home, Tasha," he said. Catching sight of a meager wag of her tail, he reached into his shirt pocket and pulled out the chlorophyll treat in its crinkling cellophane wrapper. He heard the dog's toenails dance across the porch as he tore open the wrapper and extracted its green-colored prize. Then, treat in hand, the man looked down to find the dog looking up, tail flapping frantically, eyes filled with eager forgiveness, mouth open to receive her reward.

Never a Contender

It was an assignment any cub reporter with a brain would have seen as a Big Break, a chance to shine and get noticed.

"He'll be at the airport around 5:30," my editor said, handing me a news release announcing that Norman Cousins was to speak at a local church. The church folks had arranged for us to interview Cousins at the airport. I was the night police reporter. Everyone else was tied up on other stories. This would be mine. I had about an hour to get there and meet his plane.

Norman Cousins. The name rang a bell. There'd been something in the paper recently about Cousins stepping down as editor of the *Saturday Review*, which I'd heard of and probably had seen in the library. He was stepping down to help launch a new iteration of the magazine he'd edited over the past three decades.

This was in 1972 or '73. There was no Google. No Internet. There was the newspaper morgue, to which I hustled in search of background. I found a single, skinny folder on Norman Cousins. It held a small clipping from several years earlier containing several paragraphs saying he'd be speaking to a local group. Nothing about the new magazine or anything else about him.

Well, hell, I guess I'll hafta wing it. I drove to the airport, arriving five minutes before Cousins strolled into the terminal. He looked tired. I introduced myself. He was polite. I asked him if he'd eaten. I don't remember what he said. But I hadn't eaten, so he agreed to talk to me while I grabbed something in the airport restaurant.

I remember ordering baked beans. Cousins might have gotten a cup of coffee. I remember how somber and uncomfortable he looked, just like in his photos. We sat in a booth. I was awed, in the presence of a man I knew to be a giant in the literary world, a world I aspired to be part of some day. I couldn't think of a damned thing to ask him.

We made a little polite, strained conversation. I forgot about the new magazine or even to ask the obvious questions, how it felt to be retired or was there any advice he could offer young writers or how 'bout them Yankees or what he did for cheap thrills. All I could think of was the current controversy over whether there should be "shield laws" to protect journalists who were protecting confidential sources. What did he think about that? Baffled or profoundly bored, staring at his coffee, he mumbled some clichés I pretended to write down in my reporter's notebook.

Finally, throwing in the towel, I asked him if he had a copy of the speech he would be giving that evening. From the look he gave me I might as well have called him a Republican. Still staring at me as his despair slowly lightened into irritated disappointment, he almost imperceptibly rotated his head back and forth a couple of times. At this point I'd become sufficiently alert to my disaster that I could recognize grief burgeoning at the very core of my being. Never thought to ask what he would talk about that evening. Drowned. Dead. Quit my beans. Literary giant abandoned his coffee. I paid. Went separate ways. I drove back to the newsroom and wrote a three-paragraph "story" almost identical to the one in the morgue's yellowed clipping.

That was in Iowa, where I worked as a reporter from 1970 to spring '74. From there I moved to Richmond, Virginia, and worked with the Associated Press about six months, then joined the newspaper in Newport News, where I was working when an editor told me to head up to Hopewell just south of Richmond. It was Feb. 24, 1977.

"A ship hit the Benjamin Harrison bridge," he told me. "Some cars went in the water." He said another reporter would head up through Williamsburg to the other end of the bridge, which spanned the James River. Our instructions were to call the copy desk when we had something.

As I arrived at the scene reporters were pulling in from all over Virginia and Washington, D.C. It was bedlam. Nobody knew what the hell was going on. But we all understood that if anybody had drowned in the river *that* was the story. I scouted around until I found a pay phone in the marina at the foot of the bridge. It was the only phone around. Cellular phones were still a wild-ass dream in some inventor's head.

My next job was to find somebody, anybody, who could tell me something, anything. The trick was to avoid talking to gawkers or people who only knew stuff second hand. There was at least one man shouting that he'd seen the whole damned thing. There's always one of those at every catastrophe. I lucked out when I found a young couple who had been sleeping on their boat at the marina when the ship hit the bridge over their heads.

"It was a grinding, crunching sound that went on and on," the wife said as her husband nodded agreement. Aha! This was my lead. I ran to the marina office, grabbed the phone, stuck a quarter in the slot and called my newsroom collect. I dictated what little information I had along with the quote I'd gotten from the young couple.

As I dictated, a line of reporters formed behind me. Another reporter tried to grab the phone when I hung up, but I knew him to be a jerk, so I held the phone in the air and called a friendly reporter over and gave it to him. Then I went back to the scene. When I called the newsroom about an hour later, assuring them nobody had drowned, my editor told me our report had been the first one picked up by the AP to go out on the national wire.
Yippee. That night, I turned on ABC News, figuring my story would be mentioned. I was hoping Baba Wawa would read my little report from the AP wire, but she was off that night. I got Harry Reasonable instead. But this was OK, because people had

told me my voice on the phone sounded like Harry's, so, even though he wasn't Baba, I liked Harry.

The bridge story *led* the news that night. I almost choked on my beer as Harry told us of the young couple "who heard a grinding, crunching sound that went on and on and on." Someone had added an extra "on." Maybe it was me in my excitement, or maybe the editors juiced it up a tad, or maybe it was Harry himself. Didn't matter. It gave the quote a little more resonance. A reasonable tweak, under the circumstances.

I celebrated that night. Wooeee. Next morning, the hangover was especially cruel. The bridge story led page one of the Washington Post. Wha...? My quote! Nowhere! Instead, the headline screamed something different: "I thought I was going to die!"

Bill McAllister, the Pulitzer-winning reporter who'd written the Post story, had enjoyed an exclusive interview with the bridge tender, who had hung precariously in the little tender's shack atop the bridge for several hours before he was rescued. My immediate assumption was that this was the guy I'd seen shouting for attention, that he was the bridge tender and he was so damned glad to be safe and on land he was celebrating by telling the world about it.

If so, if it was the bridge tender who was shouting at everybody. "Talk to me! I saw it all!" McAllister was the only reporter smart enough to take the guy up on it. I had watched McAllister interviewing everybody at the scene who wasn't working for a news agency. He was methodical and as thorough as a vacuum cleaner. I assumed he eventually talked to the shouting man.

Then again, maybe he was just playing poker with us. Maybe he talked to the shouter first. Knew what he had and that probably nobody else would bother, and then pretended to methodically interview all of the other potential witnesses just so the rest of us wouldn't get suspicious he already had the scoop. Then again...

Have I mentioned I never won a Pulitzer? I trust you're not surprised.

Gonzo Days

There were just the three of us at the bar. The two jockeys sat at one end, talking quietly. Occasionally Terri, the bartender, joined the conversation, her voice as muted as theirs. I sat near the other end drinking double shots of Johnny Walker Black and studying a copy of *The Daily Racing Form* I'd bought in Newport News before my 178-mile drive to Charles Town.

This was my third or fourth trip to the Charles Town Races since I'd started working as a newspaper reporter in Newport News, Virginia, in 1974. I'd picked up the racing bug in Moline, Illinois, across the Mississippi River from Davenport, Iowa, where I had my first reporting job.

It was at Moline Downs that I had become hooked on the ambience of horse racing and learned how to bet. I estimated that by the time I moved to Virginia my track losses totaled about $300. This was from  dozens of trips to the Downs and hundreds of $2 bets on individual races.

I didn't count in this total the one trip with a friend to Chicago's Arlington Park in 1973, where I lost $2 on Secretariat. I wasn't fool enough to bet against the Triple Crown winner, but by the time the race had started the odds of his winning were even. This meant the payout when Secretariat won was the same $2 I had bet. I kept the ticket and had it laminated.

I was serious about winning at Charles Town. By studying the Racing Form, which printed the day's schedules at all the major tracks, I figured I had a better chance of picking at least one long-shot to win. The Form included win-loss statistics and other information about horses in each race. My method wasn't scientific, but to my mind crunching the numbers and comparing the horses gave me a leg up to spot the horse that just might be ready to surprise the professional oddsmakers. Marginal thinking for a rank amateur, I knew, but I enjoyed the illusion.

I had just about finished drawing pencil circles around my horses on the Form when I called Terri over to order a second double Scotch. She took my order and then asked if the jockeys could borrow my Racing Form, nodding toward the other end of the bar. I glanced that way to see the two fellows smiling at me. I smiled back. "Sure," I said and added, on what for me was a reckless impulse, "and maybe you guys wouldn't mind returning the favor."

I suggested maybe they could hint which horse might be a good one to bet on. Their smiles slipped away as they looked at each other. After some murmured words, one of the jockeys turned back to me. He grinned, "I'm riding Miss Fortune in the fifth." "You gonna win?"

"I always give it my best," he said and went back to the Racing Form.

The two young men soon left. The first race would start in about half an hour. With Terri and I now the only two in the bar, she approached me with my Racing Form and another drink. "On the house," she said, setting the glass in front of me on a clean cocktail napkin.

Then she leaned on the bar and explained that my question had spooked the two jockeys. She reminded me of a scandal about a month before at a track in Maryland in which several riders were accused of fixing races. Then she told me something that started my head spinning.

"The other girl who tends bar here dates one of those two jocks. She won fifty grand last month." She gave me a conspiratorial smile before going back to her bar duties. I drank up, left her a $10 tip and headed to the track.

It was a five-minute walk, and by the time I reached the gate I knew there was something more than Scotch playing in my head. I'd done enough hallucinogens to know I was taking off on a trip. Terri most likely had slipped a little LSD in that last drink. It was common knowledge in those days that undercover narcotics police did not indulge in LSD, or "acid," because its effects were too unpredictable. Offering acid was one way drug culture people, or "heads," tested strangers who tried to buy marijuana. If the stranger was a narc he or she would give some excuse to opt out. Heads sometimes slipped acid into the drink of someone they suspected of being a narc. They called this "acid assassination."

As the "victim" of such an assassination I knew I had it made. Not only was I getting a free trip, but, when I proved I had passed the test, Terri and her friends might accept me into their circle, maybe pass me a tip on a race. Yeah, I was tripping. I stayed for a couple of races, getting higher and higher all the while, wondering just how much of the stuff she'd put in my drink. I decided to call it quits when the horses coming out of the gate were so distorted in shape and movement I wondered if I might not be able to handle myself much longer.

I walked back to the bar, my head buzzing with amplified sounds of the night and the horns and roars from the track. A different girl was behind the bar. I asked her for the other bartender, whose name at that point I didn't know.

"You mean Terri? She's off. Can I help you?" I took one of my business cards, which was embossed with the name of my newspaper and my name and phone number, and wrote: "Terri, thanks for the trip!" I handed it to the new bartender with a $10 bill. I smiled, probably way too eagerly, and left the bar.

I drove to Mabel's Motel, where I'd already paid for a room, but decided I couldn't sleep, and drove the 178 miles back to Hampton Roads through a gauntlet of trees that had come alive, their gnarled branches grabbing at my car and recoiling when I shot them the bird, laughing maniacally and shouting, "Fuck you! I'm fucking Hunter Thompson, you assholes! You got that? Hunter S. fucking Thompson!"

Next morning, after a night of no sleep, I pitched my editor the plan. We would run a little feature about the track, touting its atmosphere, to prove to Terri and her friends I was cool. Once I was in with them he and I could place the occasional bet, get rich, don'tcha know. He gave me the stinkeye. No deal.

At least he didn't fire me. Not that I was worried. You don't fire Hunter S. Thompson that easily.

To Hell With It
(fiction)

Today was probably the day. This was Whitaker's first impression, and if it *was* the day he knew he'd have to do some fast talking. If the Big Asshole was in fact going to fire him Whitaker knew he needed to muster enough power of persuasion to get the act delayed at least until his next birthday, when he would be eligible for Medicare. Things were reverting to a more primal order. Everywhere he looked, the future seemed shaky and frail. He'd already lost most of his 401 (k) with the company and had no other assets or prospects with which to keep afloat very long without his job. With no steady income he knew desperation soon would push him somewhere he was barely able to avoid imagining.

The Big Asshole had called him last night, late, as he usually did when he'd come to an important decision involving his employees. He'd started out, as always, almost deferential.

"Whit, will you be in tomorrow?" trying to sound casual, despite a self-conscious tension. Oh, shit, Whitaker thought. In? Of course he'd be in. He always went in. Every damned day. What a stupid fucking question, will he be in tomorrow.

"I was planning to, Bernie. Why, what's up?"

"I'd like to see you about nine, if that's OK." The Big Asshole's tone had cooled. Probably intentionally. The "if that's OK" was so unnecessary it reached the edge of sarcasm.

"No problem, Bernie." Whitaker was damned if he'd squirm for the Big Asshole. "Anything else?"

"No, Whit. I'll see you tomorrow. Nine."

Well, fuck you, too, asshole. He hung up the phone, opened the refrigerator next to it and found his last beer, one he'd overlooked earlier. Fuck it, he thought, wishing he had a couple more but glad for the one he found. He drank the Yuengling Black & Tan quickly, each gulp of the cold, earthy liquid flushing away more of the conversation's cloying residue.

Although the Big Asshole's voice initially had the effect of a sucker punch to the belly, as it always did on the phone even if it carried a wholly innocuous or even welcome message, Whitaker recovered immediately, projecting a tone of cautiously polite neutrality. Truth be told, his feeling toward the Big Asshole actually *was* cautiously neutral. Whitaker had no strong feelings toward him. The name "Big Asshole," was completely private, never uttered aloud. Whitaker assigned it for his own purpose merely to distinguish rank. In fact, in any context that contained a *big asshole*, there was often a *little asshole*, as well, and with the little asshole often being more deserving of the noun than the big one, the adjective served to further diminish Whitaker's assessment of the lesser person. But in this instance the Little Asshole, his supervising editor, actually was a fairly decent person. She attained asshole status merely by dint of having authority over him.

Whitaker was pushing ten when he first recognized he alone was responsible for his emotional well-being, an understanding nurtured into full bloom by a keen perception that quickly picked up on his father's sadistic passive-aggressive nature. There was never any physical abuse, just a pattern of encouraging affection and then crushing it without warning or explanation because of something the boy had said or done. At least that's what the boy had assumed. On those downsides, his father would ignore him or deny anything was wrong when Whitaker confronted him trying to clear the air. The boy saw the same thing happen to his mother, a simple-hearted timid woman with a passive personality that crumpled in bewilderment whenever her husband gave her "the silent treatment." Whitaker would try to console her as she wept alone in her bedroom. They would talk about their tormentor, wondering what they had done that was so awful. While they drew closer in these times of confusion and misery, Whitaker's own heart gradually hardened. Unwilling to allow himself to be psychologically tortured by a man who should have loved him, the boy ultimately rejected the man and turned inward for counsel. He made a conscious decision on his tenth birthday he would never again expect anything from his father, no matter how enticing the man could be.

It had to do with a bicycle, a Schwinn Black Phantom Whitaker had been coveting for months. By the time his birthday rolled around the bicycle had become an obsession. He had a newspaper delivery route, and his old bike was on its last legs. His friend Roy had gotten a Black Phantom a couple of months earlier and let Whitaker try it out. It was love at first ride. He adored everything about it - its chrome, the top grain cowhide seat, the sleek, arched lines that suggested the racing greyhound logo on the bus of that name. Love, hell. It was lust, pure and simple. Roy's was black and red. Whitaker wanted the black and green.

He'd begun lobbying for one soon after riding Roy's. He tried being subtle at first, mentioning it casually because he knew his father was big on surprises. Whitaker had learned that gift-giving occasions were best prepped by hinting at several possibilities, trying not to be too obvious which one he preferred. This could work, even if it eventually became clear which of the hints was number one because at least he was playing the game. He'd pretend to be hugely surprised even if he wasn't really, although there was always an element of surprise that he hadn't somehow offended his father so that he would deliberately give his son the gift he knew was not the one he really wanted. The boy had a certain confidence in his sense that his father wasn't deliberately cruel, that he was instead reactive, that his shutting out those closest to him was a response in the spirit of punishment for perceived transgressions undoubtedly so personal as to be embarrassing to try to explain.

Whitaker found the new Schwinn Black Phantom in his father's study three days before his birthday. The surprise and accompanying thrill approached a religious intensity. His father had draped an old Army blanket over the bicycle and had put some file boxes in front of it in an attempt at concealment, but Whitaker knew immediately what it was. He'd entered the room after making sure his mother was well into her afternoon nap. His father had gone to his gun club for some sort of shooting competition. He normally kept the door to his study locked and Whitaker normally checked the door each time he happened to pass it, with the same diligence that compelled him to poke his finger into the coin return slots of pay phones and soda machines. It was a scarcely rewarded habit, but when he did find a coin or two it seemed a vindication of some kind, a secret little bonus from the Fates.

Soon as he stepped into the sacred study Whitaker saw what he knew had to be the concealed bicycle. So certain was he of this his confidence filled the room with an electric awareness that washed back over him in a rush of conflicting sensations. There was disbelief at first, instantly overpowered by a maddening curiosity that promised ecstasy as well as a subtle dread. It was this last that blocked his compulsion to cross the room and rip back the blanket. The dread arose from a niggling notion of doubt his father had actually gotten him a Phantom, that he'd missed the point and that this bicycle was some other, lesser brand or model and Whitaker didn't want to face the disappointment were his misgivings confirmed. Nudging up from another dark crevice was a sense that if the bicycle was in fact the Phantom of his dreams and he were to uncover it now and experience the raw thrill of seeing it ahead of the appointed magic moment, his father would know, somehow would pick up the excitement no matter how diligently his son tried to suppress it. His father then of course would assume the worst, feel that his efforts to pull off an explosive surprise had been betrayed and that his own son had ruined everything. Whitaker knew he had no choice. The fates had mandated he postpone whatever was imminent - cruel, frustrated disappointment or lifetime thrill - and he resolved to wait. He paused just long enough to allow an always possible accident of fate, earthquake mayhap or quirky twist of gravity, to relieve him of the hideous suspense, then, breathing deeply and backing cautiously out of the study, he gently closed the door.

As it turned out his precautions were for naught.

On the morning of his birthday, he found the bicycle again, this time uncovered and resting on its kickstand in the middle of the living room. His parents sat on either side of it in their favorite upholstered chairs. His younger sister was playing with some toy on floor next to her mother. Whitaker's mother had awakened him with a kiss and an excited "happy birthday, Son!" before telling him there was a big surprise awaiting him as soon as he got up. He half expected to see the bicycle behind her in his bedroom, but when he saw there was nothing there, he quickly arose, brushed his teeth and entered the room where he knew the celebration would be held.

There it was, seeming as excited to see him as he it, greeting him in all its glorious Black Phantom chrome and colors. It was exactly the one he wanted. It aroused even more excitement than he'd anticipated, for an instant or two. Then he detected the gloom emanating from his father. A sidelong peek revealed a face clenched and cold, withdrawn into itself.

"Thank you, Daddy! Thank you, Mommy. Thank you thank you!" Whitaker blurted, hoping his take on his father's mood was mistaken. "It's just what I wanted!"

His father had been looking at something other than his son, staring at something behind him or through him. Without shifting his focus, he said, his voice hollow with disappointment, "It was supposed to be a surprise."

"It *is*, Daddy! I dreamed forever of getting one! It's what I wanted! It's all I ever wanted! A green and black Schwinn Black Phantom! It's a beautiful bike! Beautiful! Beautiful! Thank you! Thank you, Daddy! Thank you, Mommy! It's the best surprise I ever had!"

"You saw it in my study."

"No, Daddy! Honest, Daddy! I didn't see it! It's a surprise! Thank you thank you thank you!" But the conviction in his voice was leaching away along with the initial thrill as his father's poisonous gloom incrementally overtook the room, and this seemed to embolden his father's conviction that he was cheated of his own expected thrill from watching his son's untainted delight with the gift.

Whitaker's mother made a feeble attempt at intervention. "Dear," she started, "I'm sure…" Her voice receded into an inaudible murmur when her husband turned his head slightly in her direction, his face now a sullen fist.

It was this face that burned deepest into Whitaker's memory on that day, the image that emerged most vividly whenever he allowed his mind to drift back to what he eventually came to understand had been a defining moment for him. Without articulating it in his mind he knew beyond any challenge sentiment was a luxury he could not afford, that it interfered too easily with rational thought and that rational thought, no matter how uninformed or uncomfortable, could be his only reliable guide.

Something else happened in this crucible of awakening with his father: Whitaker looked directly without expression into his father's eyes. The boy had been conditioned to smile when he met his father's eyes, and never to hold the contact for more than part of a second. To do otherwise was to invite a frowning snarl.
"You're looking at me like I'm some kind of a bug," would be the words within the snarl. Staring at himself in a mirror after one of these chastisements Whitaker decided this reaction from his father had something to do with the color of his eyes. The irises were inky black. They contrasted with those of the rest of his family - his mother, father and younger sister - which were varied degrees of light blue. When the Star Wars movies were in vogue, people would say that Whitaker had Darth Vader eyes. He learned to use this feature to his advantage as he grew older. A police friend told him once he had the eyes of a cop.

"You stare at me long enough with those black lasers of yours and I'll confess to whatever the hell you want me to," Henry had said.

The effect of his expressionless eye contact with his father after Whitaker saw the angry face on this birthday morning was that the old man backed off. No comment about him feeling like a bug. No comment at all. The old man knew something was different now even if Whitaker hadn't completely figured it out. The self-sorry maddened fist strode purposefully from the room without a word and drove off, alone, to return late that night. Whitaker mounted his new bicycle and rode off as well, but his face beamed with joy. It wasn't quite the joy he'd anticipated but the new bike was a damned good bike and he was proud of it and the ride was a celebration of this and this alone.

His mood now as he drove through the morning traffic was less focused, more involved. A sense of do or die squirmed around an inertia of fatalism, the competitive impulse contrasting feebly with an inescapable knowledge that his career had been mediocre by any vocational measure. It didn't help the humility of this awareness to know also that the newspaper employing him was itself a flickering beacon of mediocrity, a judgment so widely shared by its staff the less reverent among them would assure each other during increasingly frequent episodes of despair that its management was "ever striving for adequacy."

Not to say that Whitaker was a bad newsman. On the reporting end of things - the digging, the cultivating of sources, the gathering of information, the nose for what is news and what is not - he was an asset, would have been a good catch for virtually any news organization. His problem was he couldn't write. Tone deaf is how one editor described this shortcoming to him early in his career. Whitaker accepted the liability but not the musical explanation. Instead, he saw his problem as similar to that of stutterers, struggling so hard to get the right word they can't settle confidently on even an obvious choice when so many nuances lingered at tongue tip. With him it was choices of narrative. The more information he had the harder he found it to organize a story, to prioritize and to make the conglomeration of details he'd gathered into an interesting sequence. Despite his decades of labor, writing sentences over and over and over atop each tower of notes as he inched his way along, his "finished stories" still brought deep sighs from copy editors before they tackled the jumble of sometimes amazing information he'd presented.

He should have been a cop, he understood now. Digging up information was all he knew how to do well. Don't have to write to be a cop. Better benefits. Henry had a decent pension and good health insurance. Too late to worry about that now. Too old to find another job at a newspaper. Too old to try private investigating or anything else that came to mind.

Shoulda been a cop. His slight build and aversion to violence notwithstanding he had the instincts of a cop. His friend was right. The stare would've served him well even if he'd had only one serious fight in his life. He had the fight about a year after his tenth birthday. It was unavoidable. Schoolyard bully sensing weakness, goaded by the stare. Bully caught off guard when Whitaker, suddenly gone berserk, landed a solid punch and kept pounding. Down went Bully with Whitaker atop, battering his tormentor bloody with diminutive fists until an adult pulled him off. The school suspended him for three days, but he returned to a new respect from everyone, stare validated and carrying a subtle emission now of danger that enabled him to continue his live-and-let-live ways without further challenge.

An indifferent chill met Whitaker when the newspaper plant came into view as he approached the overpass down ramp from the road he took between home and work his three decades as an employee there. The plain building - three stories of brown brick behind a drive-through portico at the main entrance - gave off a tinge of nostalgia instead of the usual sense of home, with its familiar bundle of concerns both trivial and large, pleasant and not for the people within along with the obligations and opportunities being one of them entailed.

As he trudged across the lot to the rear entrance he thought of his halfway promising project. It gave him a modicum of hope that if he played it right this project could strengthen his bid for six more months of health insurance, at least. The idea grew exponentially as he mounted the stairs to the second-floor newsroom lightening his step and buttressing his composure as he pushed through the door into the expanse of desks and partial cubicles where accounts of current events arrived almost continually to be talked and tapped into narratives and processed into the inky packages that fed the curiosity of about a hundred thousand local customers every day. Several copy editors were already at their desks, attention fixed on glowing computer screens. Whitaker was half an hour early for his appointment and about an hour earlier than he and most of the other reporters usually arrived.

As he walked to his desk he stole a glance through the glass wall on the newsroom side of the Big Asshole's office and saw the white shock of hair tilted toward a glowing silver computer monitor. Whitaker sat at his desk and stared at the dead screen of his own computer until he saw the BA step outside his door and look across the newsroom straight at him. When their eyes made contact the BA motioned for Whitaker that it was time. Somebody named Maxwell from Human Resources he'd seen around but never met had joined the BA. The BA crisply introduced Maxwell then settled into his leather-covered swivel chair, his back to the computer, his legs crossed at the knees. He sat like a woman,Whitaker thought. Maxwell and Whitaker sat side-by-side in leather-covered straight-backed chairs so that the three faced each other in a triangle.

"Whit, you probably know why we've called you in," the BA began.

Maxwell cleared his throat and shifted in his chair. Whitaker stared straight ahead at the BA offering no acknowledgment. The BA, dressed impeccably in a white shirt and red-and-blue striped tie, pressed chinos and shined, expensive-looking brown loafers was his usual alert, upbeat, handsome, charming self. He exuded a youthful, athletic grace and energy that suggested a man at least ten years younger, although he'd been at the paper about as long as Whitaker. Too smart to smile at Whitaker, he leaned toward him affecting an earnest concern as he awaited a response. When Whitaker remained silent the BA glanced over at Maxwell then quickly back to Whitaker.

Mathew Paust

"You know times are tough, with the economy, everywhere. Our industry especially, including this company, is no exception," he said after he realized Whitaker wasn't going to speak.

Get on with it, you asshole. I'm not stupid, Whitaker wanted to say. Instead, he said, "I was hoping you could hold off until next year. I turn 65 in January, and then I qualify for Medicare." He wanted to add, *What the fuck is six more months to a company this big, no matter how tough the times are for your bottom line?*

"Afraid we can't do that, Whit. I hate what we have to do here, but we have no choice."

"Well, can't you at least keep me on the health plan? Cut my pay in half? Cut my hours? Six months?"

"Sorry, Whit." The BA paused, looking down as though groping for a line, which would be something new for him were it true. More likely it was acting. But when he looked up his genteel features did seem different, less composed, less assertive than before. "Isn't Margaret working? Can't you join her health plan?" "Bernie, Margaret and I divorced ten years ago. Eleven."

A slap couldn't have done more to shake the BA, at least for the flash of panic that registered in his probing eyes. He recovered instantly, but his face and his manner were further softened. "I'm sorry, Whit," he murmured. "I forgot." Whitaker stared at him. Said nothing.

156

Then he remembered the file he'd brought in. "The odometer story's coming together, Bernie. I'm waiting on my Fed contact to come back with accident data. All we need is one fatal accident. I'm sure we'll find one and there may be more."

"Odometer story?"

"Yeah. I sent y'all an email a couple weeks ago. Excel Auto Sales? Buys rentals, spins the mileage back, scrubs the titles in Georgia, sells 'em as younger cars. Customer gets screwed, people get killed when the car breaks down on the road. Could be a helluva story."

"Of course. Good work, Whit. Can you type up your notes for Marie? Give her your source list?"

"I'd like to finish it myself, Bernie. I've put a lot of time in this." "Sorry, Whit. We can't keep you on any longer." The BA reached back to his desk and produced an envelope, which he handed across to Whitaker. The BA waited while Whitaker opened the envelope and removed a check.

"Ten thousand dollars? That's it? Thirty-two years I've given this company, worked hard for this company. My 401 (k)'s bled out, and you toss me overboard and give me ten thousand dollars? I'm pushing sixty-five, Bernie. I have diabetes and a bad back. What can I do with ten thousand dollars? Who the hell's gonna hire an old newspaper reporter? For anything?" He said this in an even tone. He waited a couple of seconds, then folded the check and slipped it into his shirt pocket.

The two men held each other's eyes as the BA's face gradually turned to stone. The BA stood up and offered his hand. "Maxwell has some papers for you to sign. I'll leave you two to get that done. Good luck, Whit."

Whitaker stayed seated, rotating his head as he continued to stare at the BA, ignoring the proffered hand. The BA slipped out of his office. Maxwell held out some sheets of paper, mumbling something that didn't register with Whitaker. Whitaker stood, took the papers, looked absently at them and then let them and the file he'd brought with him drop to the floor. He left the office, barely hearing Maxwell's pleas for him to come back. He left the building, climbed in his car and drove away. He drove for about an hour, aimlessly, feeling stupefied and numb, his mind operating on autopilot at a level almost out of the reach of conscious intervention. He pulled into the narrow parking lot of a familiar building, parked, got out and went in.

"Whit!" said the friendly voice of a man smaller than Whitaker, who appeared from the back of the store.

"Louie." They shook hands. It seemed they were the only two people in the store.

"A pleasure to see you, my friend. You on a story this morning? How can I help you?"

"No story, Louie. I quit the paper. Retired. At long last." He forced a smile.

"Retired, huh? Well, it's a good time to get out of the business, I think. A good time to get out of any business, huh? They say the midterm elections will change everything. Huh? Hahaha. So how can I help you today, my friend?"

Whitaker tilted his head to the rear of the store. "Still got it?"
"Ah, that! Yes! Come!" The two walked back to a display that was roped off with a discreet chain. Whitaker stared at the object of beauty it protected.

"I want to buy it," he said.

"My friend! Are you sure? The price is $3,500. I can call the owner and maybe he'll come down a little, but you should make a down payment on a new car instead, get rid of that junker you're driving."

Whitaker pulled the check out of his pocket, turned it over and endorsed the back. He handed it to Louie.

"It's a retirement bonus. I'll come get the change later. I want to take her out for a spin, right now."

In another minute, Whitaker was outside the store astride his vintage Phantom, the green, black and chrome manifestation of a time when life had seemed less complicated, easier to negotiate. He planted his feet on the pedals, gripped the rubber handlebar ends and rocked forward on the leather seat far enough to make its springs squeak. Leaning his upper body weight into his arms, he took a deep breath and felt a long nearly forgotten renewing energy surge from somewhere into his blood and through his veins. "Thanks, Louie," he said. "Thanks a million."

In another minute Whitaker and the Phantom were sailing down the street gaining speed, wind whipping past them, stripping away the years and all they contained.

Berlin Terror

Checkpoint Charlie. It sounds almost like the name of a party bar. In fact, there may well be party bars called "Checkpoint Charlie." But if there are, they're surely named after the original, which could be considered a "bar" only in the far grimmer sense of Tennyson's "Crossing the Bar," which, in the Berlin context, meant an act of final transition made by those unfortunates who were shot dead as they tried to flee the eastern, Soviet-controlled, sector to the western side and freedom.

An unlikely name for a killing ground. Charlie. It's a most casual name, a name suggestive of carefree fun: there're your good time Charlies, your Charlie McCarthys, your Charlie Browns. It exceeds in diminutiveness even the technically more diminutive of the diminutives for "Charles," that being "Chuck," which sounds almost too inside baseball for someone outside the game. Nope, "Charlie" is for every occasion, except maybe for being gunned down while trying to dash or sneak across the football-field-length of pitted pavement that separated the communist guard shacks from those of the Western allies.

The "Charlie," incidentally, came from the NATO phonetic alphabet for "C." In retrospect, "Checkpoint C" might have had a closer emotional connection with the high and low drama ever playing on that stretch of political stage from 1959 until 1989, when the Wall came down.

I walked across that patch of "no man's land" into what was then East Berlin in 1970. A couple of hours later I was surrounded by a rifle squad and herded into the back of a canvas-covered military truck. Watching these hard-faced young men, who looked to be in their early teens, rack back the bolts on their weapons, which I'm thinking were probably Stg-44 assault rifles inherited from the *Wehrmacht* of WWII, definitely got my attention.

They jumped out the back of the truck, which had rumbled up and screeched to a stop about a block or two from the *Reichstag* ruins, toward which I and three companions were walking. The whole scene was strange. There had been no traffic on the streets-neither vehicular nor pedestrian-throughout our stroll in the city.

The only commercial outlets I recall were a bookstore, where I bought a beautifully bound English-Russian dictionary for a fraction of what I would have paid in the West, and a drab restaurant where someone in uniform guarded the door until the four of us had given the manager every German mark, U.S.

dollar and cent in our possession in order to pay the unspecified "cost" of our meal of cold cuts, cheese and fruit juice.

The Cold War was in full chill. I had gotten out of the Army three years earlier and was bumming around Europe at the time. I was in West Berlin expecting to meet a couple of friends from home - one, a college buddy and the other a fellow I'd grown up with. Our schedules didn't jibe, however, and we never got together behind the Iron Curtain. Meanwhile, I decided to visit East Berlin on my own.

It was a cool morning, I recall, but I can't remember the month. Checkpoint Charlie was within walking distance of my hotel, which was within view of the imposing Brandenburg Gate, with its Doric columns and horse-pulled chariot atop. I spent about half an hour at Charlie, walking through the little museum that featured photos of people shot to death a few yards away as they'd tried to escape to the West. I remember a small automobile in the museum, which had an ingenious hidden compartment for smuggling escapees to the West. It didn't fool the Soviets.

While touring the museum I met the three young people with whom I then crossed over to the Eastern sector for what we anticipated would be a leisurely tour of the forbidden city. My little group included two U.S. college girls, who were enjoying a "junior year abroad," studying in London, and a young British male student.

Our little jaunt screeched to a halt, however, when the military truck stopped next to us and the rifle-toting teenagers hopped out and surrounded us. The two girls immediately began crying when a smallish man in a gray-green uniform approached and demanded, in German, our passports. This prompted a running argument with the British lad, who spoke the host language quite well. But he gained no ground, despite sounding fairly sure of himself and nearly as authoritative as the smallish man, whose manner and uniform insignia indicated that he was the leader - I'm guessing a non-commissioned officer of some sort.

This authoritative fellow ordered us into the back of the truck.

We complied, as the troops - about six or eight of them - motioned with their rifles the direction we should go. I had just sat down on one of the wooden planks that served as seats along each side of the truck when the leader barked out my name. For the first time during the incident I noticed a prickling sensation ripple along the hairs on the back of my neck.

"*Herr Paust! Raus mit du!*" came a shout, ordering me out of the truck. I complied. The little man then strutted around from the truck cab, where evidently he'd been sitting and going through our passports, and handed mine back. He waved me away. The troops then climbed into the back of the truck - the girls were wailing by now, and the Brit was still shouting and scolding in the language of his captors - their leader returned to the cab and the truck rumbled off.

I stood there alone on the deserted sidewalk holding my passport, which, I noticed, had "foreign service" stamped across my photo. I'd gotten it when I was stationed in Germany with the Army. Nuts, I thought, they think I'm some kind of spy, and any second now a black limo will screech up beside me and I'll be hustled off to God knows where for God knows how long.
I began walking briskly, while trying to appear nonchalant, back the several blocks to Checkpoint Charlie. I made it, without seeing a single motor vehicle or pedestrian. It was as if I were in a movie based on a story by the Czech nightmarist Franz Kafka. OK, I figured, this is where they will nab me. They were simply waiting for me to arrive.

They weren't. I made it through the gauntlet of East German and Russian border guards without incident, although one of the Russians made a small joke out of the fact that I'd grown a scruffy beard since my passport photo was shot. I reported the incident to the U.S. MPs, and waited on a bench outside the guard shack for about an hour before I saw the truck rumble up to the gate on the Soviet side and my erstwhile companions climb down and walk through the checkpoint to join me on the bench.

The girls were still crying, and the Brit was still indignant, although now he spoke English.

He said he and the girls were delivered to the "VoPo" (*Volks Polizei*, i.e People Police, no kumbaya) equivalent of a precinct station where the East German equivalent of a magistrate berated them for looking scruffy. Indeed, the youngsters had the slightly unkempt appearance associated back then with "hippies," the Brit, especially, with full beard and uncombed hair down to his shoulders. I believe he or one of the girls wore a blanket or serape-type garment. I wasn't especially kempt myself, but my hair and beard were shorter. And I had that "foreign service" stamp on my passport mugshot.

We stopped somewhere nearby for a beer. The girls' emotional expressions eventually eased back to sniffles, the Brit's indignation relaxed a tad, we promised to write and we went our separate ways.

Suspense
(fiction)

I am dead as a doornail, as my dad would say. It never occurred to me when I was a kid and still listing to him to wonder at this analogy. I couldn't have told anyone what a doornail was, although I vaguely recall at least once picturing in my mind a large, sturdy nail like those old-fashioned boxy kind wedged in remnants of long ago carpentry.

My interest in what a doornail might be never rose above that tentative association, a half-hearted nod to its prospects as a curio displaced, no doubt for the better, by modern materials. If the origin of my dad's expression remained elusive, its import never came into question. Simply, dead as a doornail meant dead. Not dead tired or dead to the world, not a little bit dead or nearly or maybe or probably dead. Just dead. All the way, no doubt about it, completely and absolutely irreversibly and usually regrettably forever and evermore dead. As dead as I am as you read this.

I can say this because of where I am and what I see before me. Strapped inside my crumpling Nissan Sentra is where I am, rather, hanging in the seat belts of my upside down crumpling Nissan. The crumpler in this instance is an International Harvester truck, into the path of which my Nissan came to rest after skidding out of control and rolling across a grass median.

A frothy garnet spew blots most of the truck's gnashing grill, which leered at me an instant prior with enough karmic glee to fill an eternity, an epiphany of sorts to discover comfort in a display of one's own arterial blood as a shield from the slayer's profanity. It took working back with logic from this vision to discover that what at first struck me as an impossibly shaped, glowing shadow, an amoebic hologram frozen in mid-pulse before my eyes was in fact what it was, sprung into its geyser by the Nissan's steering wheel, which had been shoved far enough into my mouth to detach the jaw and rip open a carotid. I eventually deduced that the grungy steel-filled rubber arc would conclude its lunge all the way through my spine into the filthy seat fabric above my shoulders and perhaps beyond.

This enlightenment occurred quite a bit later, an eon or so after the gushing gore first came into view. It's taken much deliberation for me to be leaning now toward the blood-fright theory as an explanation for my predicament. Scared I was. No doubt about that. Ever increasingly so during the several seconds leading up to the blood. The approach of panic brought a proportional elongation of time outside my mind, which developed inversely to the velocities of my thought sequences. It's a psychological phenomenon I suspect relates to the cinematic illusion of slow motion. The more frames of film exposed to a particular motion the slower the motion appears on a screen if the projected film reel revolves at its standard rate. The greater the racing mind exceeds the speed of whatever motion it perceives, the more increments of that motion are apt to register. We are told that the Devil is in the details. That very well may be, folks. It just may well be.

Any concept of hell that I entertained before now - I use *now* in an objective sense here quite distinct from my impression that all time outside my mind has stopped dead in its tracks - is poignant, callow in its meek reflection of the fire that roasts the soles of my soul these relentless millennia.

The physical pain was easiest to get past, nonexistent, in fact, until I remembered that what was happening to me surely must hurt. It did, then, of course, excruciatingly, but I quickly caught on to the power of focus and how I could use it to shift my attention to something other than the howls of nerve endings torn from each other or the screams of others being stretched to their limits. Among these are the network of nerves that service my larynx, enough of which remains intact to the extent that it conveys my terror with the traditional squeal, registering in my eternal moment as a jagged itch that reaches up from the killing zone into the adenoids.

I use *eternal* to convey a probability, which, if I've not come quite fully to accept as conclusive at least has won sufficient corroboration by the perceived eons of my situation that neither of the logical alternatives interests me: scene ekes back into motion or instant oblivion. I'm long prepared for either.

This may seem odd in that I've come to believe the credit for my cerebral fandango goes to a primal fear of dying, that the prospect of death was so unacceptable at that instant that its imminence could not be denied in the usual ways yet was nonetheless managed in a punch of mind to warp speed, keeping denial ahead of demise.

Chemistry of desperation. I know it from my attention deficit disorder, genius at diversion right up to crunch time and then panic-fueled manic focus. Adrenalin junkie, now telepathist.

Telepathist. That you're reading this proves as much, although I can only speculate how I've come to engage the typist. Yet, who better to fly fancy than someone with all the time in the world and nothing to do but cogitate? Getting used to the notion that I have become an endless, helpless flame of consciousness, that oblivion for me is utterly out of reach if not out of the question, is an exhausting process, or would be in the usual context where energy matters.

Somebody told me that an LSD trip is triggered by the microsecond it takes the brain to react to the chemical, that all of the cerebral pyrotechnics and optical and aural distortions that spin out for sometimes hours emerge from the cornucopia of that single spark of chemical effect. The idea fascinated me at the time, but I made no effort to explore its plausibility. I'm inclined to wonder now if it wasn't balderdash if only because I doubt that any scientific analyses done in the early 1970s of how hallucinogens affect the brain would have gone much beyond the anecdotal. Surely not to the extent of measuring actual chemical/brain interactions. Even if anything so sophisticated were being done back then it is unlikely any of the drug adventurers I came across would have known about it. Probably bubbled up during some pharmaceutical fueled soiree. It tickled my fancy then, and from my immeasurably expanded *a priori* vantage seems tenable to me now.

There've been long moments in my current state when I welcomed, when I begged for the ending of this long, strange trip. An endless sleep promises an end to more than the physical and mental torments, which I have learned to manage. I have become fascinated by the prospect of conclusion. Suspense has always irritated me. It corrupts me, taunts me with its reminder that I'm at a mercy beyond my reach. Remembering the suspicion that I'm the one wielding the mercy brings a desolation of spirit palpably worse than any other of my hells. I remember it often. There was a time, a long, long stretch extending from when it first came to me, that the possibility I am my own Inquisitor stunk up every hairline crack in every thought. Getting past it was complicated, fraught with more subtle twists and unacceptable inferences than the standard job performance evaluation. It ultimately came down to - it surprised me no end when I finally understood that this was it - getting comfortable with myself.

I had always been annoyed by, and at the same time susceptible to folks who exude the kind of innocence that bespeaks a complete unconditional acceptance of self, an acceptance so unquestioning it might have survived unscathed the trials of Job, an impervious buoyancy that keeps the head above the water no matter how wicked the turbulence it rides.

I never parsed it out then, but I see now that my resentment grew out of a suspicion that linked the ease I perceived with smugness. I used to joke that attaining smugness was my life's goal. As with most jokes it was half true. I wanted to be happy, but I sensed the only way I could attain happiness would be to believe I was in fact happy, which would require me to embrace folly, to become, not just to play, the fool, gladly, and I consistently doubted I would ever find the power of concentration to do so. Drink or the occasional recreational drug could give me illusory moments, but this grace was all too fragile when it came, too easily perforated by the ubiquitous misgiving. I envied those who seemed to be bringing it off, and I resented my envy.

I was missing the point of view, of course. Any parish priest, rabbi, guru or imam could have shown me my error: too much attention to wanting, not enough to gratitude. A bit late for me to be catching on to this, you might think, as did I initially, yet it has held up. The word *gratitude* keeps its currency, has a calming, renewing capacity even in the abstract, just bringing it to mind with no particular context.

Its constancy is a mystery such that in trying to get to the bottom of it I've developed a theory along the lines of a finite saturation point of gratitude, if you will, which, when it is reached a transcendence occurs. I've pressed toward that saturation point, swooning with an all-encompassing spirit of gratitude, throwing myself to the winds of gratitude, setting myself adrift on a sea of gratitude, making gratitude my mantra, becoming gratitude, testing the damned theory to either debase gratitude or ride it to deliverance. I know, I know, it's the motive that foils me. I'm curious that gratitude thus far is no more than what it's been, and I'm grateful it's been no less.

Madness occupies much of my attention. I found it at first an escape from the implications of my predicament. Shrieking, wailing, giggling, voiceless, of course, yet undeniably aural. Eventually the signals from my forsaken soul lost their relevance along with the presumptive demand for relevance. Madness now comes in little flicks and flashes, inevitable nips from the philosophic gnats and the occasional horse fly. These micro-assaults arrive not in patterns, which could aid insight, but frequently enough to boggle the promise in any promising notion.

Demons pursue even as I nap, which is how I regard the infrequent episodes of passivity when I am surrendered completely to music. Most often I hear Mozart. My musical taste had been eclectic, if uninformed. I can recall owning only one Mozart album, which gave me sustenance on many an eve of college exams.

In my present state at first I hadn't a clue as to which compositions were on the album or which orchestra performed them, information that became accessible as I became more at home in my mind, learned to plumb it archival intricacies. As the album replays for me now I am struck by how invariably I find something fresh, some nuance that reaches me for the first time, no matter how often I've heard the same recording. I have the sense that Mozart's mind is suspended as well, as alive as mine and merging with mine as if, utterly acquiescent though I feel while listening, something of me is joining the music, helping in some undeliberate, osmotic way with its creation.

Images often appear when this is happening. It's Winona Ryder during the Divertimento in D Major finale, whirling on a ballroom floor, black eyes flashing, impertinent face floating above an impossibly complicated assemblage of elegant Victorian fabrics. At some point I'm whirling with her, her eyes so near mine I can see one of her pupils deliver a lascivious wink.

Then comes the intrusion, when it comes. Most recently it was a mosquito alighting on the tip of Winona's joyous nose. A smirk on the intruder's narrow face resembled that of a former employer. At other times it's a noise, a sneeze, a fart or an odor: fart, halitosis, stale deep-fry grease, bubblegum. On one of these occasions my ex-boss, full bodied and unwinged, cut in on Winona and whirled a time or two with me. These and a myriad other myopic insults arrive often enough during my reveries with Winona that latent annoyance lurks every time nonetheless. A mocking syncopation all the more irritating for its failure to so much as scratch Mozart's majesty.

But you don't need me to tell you that. Listen to a proficient rendering of the D Major Divertimento, the finale, seven billion, twelve million, four hundred eighty six thousand six hundred and eleven times or so, and you can see for yourself. If you can find the July 29, 1985 Henry Wood Hall recording by the London Sinfonia, maybe my ex-boss will whirl with you, as well.

I don't wish to leave the impression it's just the Mozart that starts playing at these nap times. Another regular is Miles Davis's Bitch's Brew, a smoky, quietly screaming late night alchemy that had always been a perfect drinking companion. Hearing its shrieks and stalking beat invariably harks me back to those nights of sauce and solitude, rolling the same riddles around the skull as then but no longer hinting at solutions. The Brew is now largely style, its poignancy at each arrival carrying incrementally less mystique. I'm persuaded that the glimpse of soul Miles ultimately renders is more agreeable than he'd have liked.

Expanding this notion toward the universal, I suspect eonian scrutiny can leaven all but the subtlest manifestations, that they might be held dispassionately. I suspect that should I reach this point and beyond, to include the subtlest manifestations, then, possibly, whatever has kept the Nissan's steering wheel from completing its trajectory will lose its impetus and I shall sleep at last the sleep beyond Miles and Amadeus. I am fairly dispassionate about the prospect, but it still tickles.

I'm occupied of late fielding questions. A blizzard of questions, actually, Does everyone end like this? Am I a fluke? So long as I think, I am? Or is it *can* everyone end like this, perhaps depending on attitude? If I don't know I'm dying - bullet in the back of the head, stroke - does my mind behave as it is now? Is there in every brain an all-powerful circuit linking every body cell and poised to fire up and take control at the catastrophic instant?

Despite the impossibility of my ever knowing if this message gets through, I'm intrigued by the thought that it shall, no matter how remote the odds.

In an infinite realm, the possible is the rule. Insanity has overtaken me many, many times in this timeless state as I've struggled to escape the posit that if everything that's possible must in fact exist then everything that exists must exist in infinite numbers and variations. As you pluck a hair from your head there is an infinite number of you in the universe plucking that same hair from their heads, while an infinite number of you are plucking a different hair, and an infinite number of you are plucking no hairs, and the pluckers are plucking an instant ahead of and behind you and two instants and three and on and on. I expect this will drive me mad many, many more times, perhaps an infinite number of times, but right now I am looking at it with the cognitive counterpart of glazed eyes.

Simultaneously, it amuses me to imagine the infinite varieties of myself and of the jackasses who pulled in front of me and the shades of difference in what I did and what they did (and are doing and will do) to make this come out otherwise.

Several seconds either way in my morning routine, or in theirs, and we would have missed each other. A little brighter or quicker on their part, or less irritable on mine. On theirs, to wait until I had passed the intersection before pulling out; on mine, had I gotten laid the night before or that morning I'd have let it go instead of cursing and deliberately coming up fast behind them to teach them a lesson. Had I had the cocoa instead of the coffee for breakfast I might have allowed their inexcusably mindless driving pass without censure and its concomitant retaliation.

Had I then remembered the trick I'd recently discovered for thwarting limbic ambushes of my neocortex, the incantation that seemed to be working to head off emotional seizures and supplant them with calming reason, I might have arrived at work as usual to do whatever the routine was that I did.

I remember even now the incantation that had struck me as so promising when it came to me on a strip of paper from a fortune cookie, but of which I was unmindful when it might have saved me from this ambiguous eternity. A sequence of simple imperative sentences: *Be still. Be patient. Be brave. Abide. Forgive. Love.*

When I first read them, the almost hypnotic ability of this succession of words to lower my pulse rate and clear my mind eluded explanation. I since surmised that their influence derived from focusing attention on particular anatomical sensors. *Be still* spoke to the lower part of my brain, the robotic thalamus, which shoots emotional demands up the pipeline. The next two commands interceded further along the reactive network, soothing and reassuring tendrils the first had set atwitter. *Patience*, the promise that stillness was not abandoned. *Bravery*, reaching higher to the frontal lobes, reminding that dignity won't be denied. *Abide*, another promise, this one that suffering need not be in vain. *Forgiveness*, of course, is a demand on the cortex proper, this vaulted sanctuary of understanding, an ethereal realm where ideas appear and vie for favor, the only human terrain where communion with a greater consciousness is possible. And, finally, *Love*. Magic *Love*, allowing only the wholly surrendered to enter, and then embodying the self, wholly.

My strategic error was not taping the strip of paper from the cookie onto my dashboard. I had taped it somewhere, probably on my computer monitor at work or on the one at home. I imagine it had either lost its novelty or hadn't become imbedded in my mind sufficiently to be there when I needed it most. Else I'd have thought, or even spoken: *Be still*, when the rage first broke upon me as I grasped that the other car (I never got a good look at it, but I've fixed in my emotional memory that it carried at least three old people.) had pulled in front of me and was going too slow for me to avoid having to take measures to keep from ramming it.

Had I remembered *Be still*, and not been so inattentive myself as to not consider that the roads had become slick from the drizzle I'd have taken my foot off the accelerator and eased around them in gentle spirit. Moreover, had I allowed for the possibility of their unwanted good intentions (I lumped them together as co-conspirators) I'd have whipped around them sooner, instead of waiting until the final seconds to frighten them, when an instant after I started into my whip they started easing into the same lane into which I was whipping.

And had I allowed for the possibility that these elders were less sluggish than I assumed, I'd have continued trying to get around them on the theory they'd stop drifting into my lane once they saw what I was doing, which is what they did, being so polite as to begin drifting back into the original lane, just as I whipped back into it, leaving me the only remaining maneuver: a jerk of the wheel that sent my car spinning toward the grassy median whereupon it bounced, rolled and scraped along on its top into the path of the truck.

I had my final glimpse of the car that had pulled in front of me as my right rear wheel tripped on the median curb. The other car seemed to be accelerating now. I imagined its occupants watching my demise with a touch of fascination and relief we hadn't collided. I suspected the fleeing car was aglow with a sense of that grateful tingle old folks surely enjoy while watching a reckless punk getting what he deserved.

I wonder who they are. They might be turning around to come back and try to help me. They might be folks I knew or who knew me. I wonder if the truck driver got out of this, or if a moment after me he, too, or she, was suspended in dying mind. It's all wonder now.

Lessons? Not sure. Maybe analogy: Take the discipline of a football player, a quarterback or receiver. You know you're going to get hit, but you concentrate on doing your job as if you won't. Stretch to pull the ball out of its trajectory while enforcing absolute denial of the inevitable impact of a significant part of a ton of hurtling, hysteria-driven meat and bone desperate to crush the life out of you. More complex, standing in the pocket, surveying a field of predatory tonnage bent on smashing you as you strive to identify a viable distant target and connect with it before the essentially inevitable crunch.

The concept of second efforts fits well here, too, the juking and spinning, the charging ahead, the scrambling to your feet and persisting after being slammed to the ground, the persisting, no matter how bleak seem the odds, right up until the play is whistled dead or until the game clock reaches four zeros. Games showcase the power of attitude over performance. Where the analogy can't keep up with us is its comfort factor. Winning isn't everything, said Vince Lombardi, it's the only thing. If life were a game, we'd all let the coach down, ultimately.

Norman Mailer wrote that it's all about courage outweighing cowardice in the balance. I liked this idea until it became clear Mailer probably held his liquor better than I. The line too easily blurred for me between brave and foolhardy, chicken and cunning. Mailer thought to settle these quandaries through existential deliberation.

I went on the wagon.

Flying Too High

I was 7 or 8, too young to understand enough of what was going on to remember any but the most salient details. For me this meant the odd visual or expectation or, in one instance, disappointment. For the sake of a smoother narrative I intend to guess at some of the less salient details without qualifying which are guesses and which have been retrieved from my brain's hard drive.

Key players were my dad, my mother's brother-in-law and several members of the local Kiwanis club who were also friends of my parents. The time was summer, 1948 or '49.

The event was a fund-raising production of the 1930 musical *Flying High*. On Broadway the cast included Bert Lahr, Kate Smith, Oscar Shaw and Grace Brinkley. The following year it came out as a movie, again with Bert Lahr but now casting Charlotte Greenwood, Pat O'Brien, Charles Winninger and Hedda Hopper as the other main characters.

My Wisconsin hometown, for which signs at the city limits announced a population of 2,500, had to come up with its own casting solution, as all the club had purchased were the one-time production rights, scripts and scores and some basic props. With an unwritten males-only membership rule at the time, the club had no choice but to cast the musical's female roles with Kiwanians in drag. These included my uncle and several family friends.

Not that anyone had to drag these civic-minded gents onto the auditorium stage on the top floor of City Hall in their wives' clothes. They were eager to do it. The whole town was eager to see it. At least this was the plan. Not for my dad. He would be the emcee introducing the play to the audience. My dad had another reason to be eager about *Flying High*.

He would be promoting the event by flying over our town in his Piper Cub and dumping several dozen little bags of ballast with parachutes attached that would drift down and dazzle the townspeople with the promise of a free ticket inside several of the bags.

My dad owned a succession of little airplanes during my childhood. He kept them at a grassy airstrip on the edge of town that ran alongside a cow pasture. Flying, he often told us, was his substitute for a psychiatrist. "When I'm up there looking down on everything all the stuff that's been bothering me just goes away," he would say. He might have believed it, but we knew better. When he couldn't look down on us from his airplane, he'd look down his nose at us and everyone else on the ground. But that story's not nearly so much fun as this one.

The plane from which he would bomb our town with the promotional packets was a little yellow two-seater. He enlisted the rest of the family to help get the packets ready. This meant my mother and me, as my sister was old enough then merely to watch. Come to think of it I might not have been much help with this work either, but I do remember the rows of paper bags on the dining room table into which "we" poured some sand and packed a flier-ha-ha advertising the show. Several of the fliers also had tickets attached. Then "we" twisted the top of each bag shut and secured it with piece of string into which was inserted the string "shroud lines" of a tissue parachute.

My mother, whose fingers were more than adequately deft for this type of work, undoubtedly did the heavy twisting and inserting. She also carefully stuffed the finished packets into a couple of burlap bags she'd gotten from her farmer sister. My dad was all grins when he loaded the burlap bags into the car on Friday morning for the drive to the airstrip. His "bombing mission" had been duly advertised in the local newspaper and on the local radio station. The curtain for *Flying High* was scheduled to rise the following evening.

This was summer so I was home from school. I volunteered to ride with my dad and help him dump the packets, but he wisely told me there would be no room. The burlap bags would fill the spare seat, behind his. He would have to empty them out the window himself.

About an hour after he left for the airstrip we heard his airplane and ran outside to see him circling overhead. We strained to see if we could spot what we assumed would be a cloud of tiny colored dots blossoming out from the yellow plane. Nothing. After circling a few more times, he flew away.

A weary gloom was clouding his face when he arrived home. We didn't see anything, we said, not helping the mood.

"They all blew over by the marshes." His voice affected an unusual analytic detachment. "I should have gone further west, maybe. And I was too high."

No one ever reported finding any of the packets.

The show was a hoot.

Grandma Should have Carried

I had mixed feelings when The Misfit leveled his pistol and blew Grandma to Kingdom Come in Flannery O'Connor's *A Good Man is Hard to Find*. First, that's a helluva way to treat a grandma – any grandma, even a hypocritical pseudo-Christian dingbat who brings murder upon her family and herself because she can't keep her damned yammering mouth shut. A burst of laughter escaped my throat, against my better nature, when The Misfit tells his sidekick Bobby Lee, "She would of been a good woman if it had been somebody there to shoot her every minute of her life."

 The Misfit, who saw through Grandma's bullshit from the start, meant that when she realized she couldn't talk him out of shooting her too, after hearing his associates shoot her son and his family to death in a nearby woods, she finally shut the hell up. Christian interpretations differ, of course, some seeing her finding the grace she'd been faking all along, or, as others more charitably put it, finding the grace she'd been *seeking* all along.

My problem with this view is the notion that grace means you're obliged to go docile and surrender to blissful acceptance while some jackass points a loaded pistol at your chest and pulls the trigger. I can buy this idea if I'm left with no other choice. If I'm bound hand and foot, say, or totally paralyzed, incapable of any physical resistance, then I would prefer to reach a state of mind that would enable me to meet my inevitable fate with at least an illusion of grace and dignity and a manageable level of fear. No begging or screaming, no crapping my pants until I'm actually dead. This type of mental discipline or Zen *jiu jitsu* takes years to master, I imagine, leaving one to decide if it's worth the trouble on the off chance some jackass some day will render you helpless and then put a bullet in your heart.

Better to even the odds with your own pistol, to my way of thinking. Say Grandma had been toting a snubnose .38 in her handbag when the family's car wrecked on a country road and they were approached by The Misfit, a notorious murdering prison escapee and his two cohorts. Having the pistol would tell us right off Grandma wasn't as stupid as she seemed, which would either heighten the tension or jerk the story from its pedestal as an ambiguous, dark literary piece and leave it as just another shoot-em-up with the good guys having an even chance. Either way, with my insertion of a pistol in Grandma's bag, instead of shrieking, scrambling to her feet and proclaiming, "You're The Misfit! I recognized you at once!" thus sealing the family's fate, she more likely would have waited for an opening, a chance to get the drop on the three killers, and then, with the kids and their parents safely behind the cover of their car or behind trees in the nearby woods, she could have whipped out her .38 and opened up an entirely new set of options.

"Drop yore shootin' irons and git on yore knees, you dirty rat murderin' scoundrels!" she might have ordered, training the deadly barrel in her two-handed grip at The Misfit's head, perhaps even thumbing back the hammer with a loud click for effect. Were she the good Christian she claimed or tried to be and the wanted felons had complied with this no-nonsense granny's instructions, all might have ended happily for the bumpkin family, who, after the killers were arrested and taken away, would have had stories to tell and perhaps write for the rest of their lives. Grandma's feisty face would have been front and center on newspaper front pages hither and yon. The local Chamber of Commerce would have named her citizen of the decade. Hell, she could have been elected mayor of her town, for life.

In another scenario, she might simply have shot the stinking rat bastards dead. The law likely would have smirked and winked, her fame have enjoyed the spice of titillating news photos of the bloody corpses she'd made and her local priest have tut-tutted whilst gently delivering her from any ecclesiastical consequences of her non-sanctified interpretation of the Sixth Commandment and Sunday dinners at the family's home would have taken on a whole new ambience.

But Grandma, as Ms. O'Connor tells us, was unarmed at the time of her meeting The Misfit and his cut-throat attendants. Her only weapon was her mouth and a less than persuasive knowledge of biblical assurances. She tried charm, which The Misfit brushed off with patronizing sneers. She tried blunt-force religion, claiming Christ could save even The Misfit. This angered The Misfit, who countered that because he had not seen Christ perform any miracles he couldn't believe any had happened. Finally she reached out and touched him on the shoulder.

O'Connor tells us, *The Misfit sprang back as if a snake had bitten him and shot her three times through the chest. Then he put the gun down on the ground and took off his glasses and began to clean them.*

If the Woodsman is Late

Versions of the Little Red Riding Hood fable have been frightening children, especially girls, since at least a century before Columbus planted the Spanish flag in the Bahamas. In many of these versions the ending is not happy for Riding Hood

or her grandma, as the wolf, later known as The Big Bad Wolf, eats them both. These versions were intended to scare the bejeebies out of kids, impressing upon them the importance of avoiding strangers and staying the hell out of deep dark woods.

The rescuing Woodsman doesn't appear until a couple of centuries down the road. In one of the first versions with him as hero he does not arrive upon the scene until after the wolf has eaten the two, but because they were swallowed whole the Woodsman frees them – still alive, of course – by slicing open the wolf's belly. The three – Riding Hood, Grandma and the Woodsman – then fill the wolf's belly with stones, and when the foul creature awakens and is thirsty from his "big meal" he waddles to the well, falls in and drowns. In later versions the Woodsman rescues Riding Hood by hearing her screams and arriving in the nick of time as she flees Grandma's house with the wolf, wearing Grandma's nightgown, close behind. The Woodsman chops the wolf to pieces. Grandma, who had been hiding in the closet, comes out and joins the celebration.

That's the basic story my mother read to me before I wore long pants. There are more recent versions, some in which Riding Hood seduces the wolf and others in which she and the Woodsman are close close friends at the beginning of the story and in which Grandma's role is too complicated to bother with at the moment. The point I'm building to here, which is hinted at in the title, is that unless the Woodsman is at Riding Hood's side at all times she's fairly helpless in the event a hungry wolf with a yen for the flesh of a tender young maiden eyes her all alone, especially if she's taking a break in the deep dark woods whilst on her way to Grandma's house with a basket of goodies.

What if the Woodsman, then, is not in attendance, but asleep under the tree against which his ax is propped, too far away to hear his beloved's shriek of terror should the wolf pop out from behind a tree bearing evil intent? Or at least too far away to awaken and schlup to where it seemed the shriek emitted from in time to bring this tale to a happy denouement? What if his ardor for Ms. Hood had cooled, his heart found someone else? What if? There are hundreds of them, perhaps thousands of what ifs that could interfere with Riding Hood's rescue from the snarling, befanged, drooling beast that looms before her.

Of course, were she packing, had she slipped a 9mm Beretta into her basket before tripping down the path into the deep dark woods, then surely a different outcome could be anticipated. Let me tell you something. That's what I would have in *my* basket were I wearing a cute little skirt and a bright red cap on my jaunt through the deep dark woods to Grandma's house or anywhere else. That way, were I to tire midway along my jaunt and decide to sit a spell under the canopy of a big oak tree, leaning my back against its rough, protective trunk, I'd be ready in case a big bad anything popped out and confronted me with ill designs. As they say on the mean streets of the city, speaking of caps, I'd be ready to pop right back at my would-be molester.

As they say in the comfy suburbs of the city, when seconds count, help is only minutes away. Unless, of course, you're prepared to help yourself.

Tough Enough?

The older I get the more I worry about the important things, the life changers. Buying my first house marked the start of this new look at values. From then on, the prospect of being sent by my newspaper to Nags Head when hurricanes threatened no longer stimulated the adrenalin of adventure. Now, I hoped someone else would get that assignment. The prospect of losing my own home took all of the fun out of looming disasters.

Fun was in very short supply the second week of September, 2003, as my community braced itself for the arrival of the season's biggest hurricane, a category five monster raging across the Atlantic on an arc that included Virginia in its landing zone. We'd been threatened by other hurricanes since my move to Gloucester in 1978, but none had given us more than a light brush before arcing up the coast and back out to sea. The forecasts for this one, dubbed "Isabel" by the National Weather Service, offered no such comfort. The storm's predicted track never wavered as the hurricane's rotating mass of lethal winds closed in on our coast.

For the first time since I'd bought the house I screwed sheets of plywood into the window frames. My wife and our kids arranged to stay with friends up-county from our lowland neighborhood, which invariably experienced some flooding during heavy rains. With the storm's landfall imminent, my editors assigned me to spend the night at a local firehouse to report how the volunteers coped with potential catastrophe. We herded our six or seven cats into the house before we abandoned it for the night.

My world flipped upside down and around and around the night of Sept. 18 as I lounged on a cot in the firehouse trying to make sense of the crackling radio chatter from the county's emergency dispatcher. One of the calls began to dominate our attention as it developed into a harrowing narrative of a family stranded on the roof of their house as floodwaters rose around them. The house was less than a mile from mine.

I rode with the ambulance crew that headed out to rescue them. We followed a ladder truck that tried to lead us through a flooded intersection as we neared the stricken family. The fire truck couldn't get through, so we had to turn back. An Army National Guard vehicle with a higher wheel base tried, as well, and failed. Eventually a sheriff's deputy and a state trooper reached the family by wading through rushing water that reached their armpits. They'd gotten near the floating rooftop in a small boat, which they used to bring the family to safety.

Next morning the sun was out and the air was still. Isabel had moved inland and away from us. When the tide went out and the flooding receded from the major roads, I headed home, my stomach sick with dread over what I might find. We'd received reports by then of entire homes in my neighborhood swept away into the York River during the night. Utility trucks, many of which had come from neighboring states and as far as Georgia, blocked the end of my road. Falling trees had pulled power lines down, and this debris had to be cleared before I could get home. When at last the road was clear, sometime that afternoon, my dread grew exponentially with each house I passed toward the other end of the road, where we lived. Relief whooshed out in a massive sigh when I saw our little bungalow still standing and apparently undamaged.

Floodwaters had risen to within a hair of entering the house through our front door. The cats, scared but safe, feigned indignation. I lost manuscripts and books from my office in a converted garage, and the flooding had ruined some heirloom photos and garden and lawn equipment in another outbuilding.

We were without power several days, and the cleanup took weeks. We've moved since to higher ground, but some families are still living in FEMA trailers in the old neighborhood.

A week before Isabel, I wouldn't have thought I could handle even this relatively minor disruption of our lives. That we did, that we adapted overnight to an uprooting of our equanimity and that we coped and got on with our lives has given me a new comfort of mind I wouldn't have imagined before then.

I've returned to a softer, more comfortable life. I don't want to have to go through something like Isabel again. Yet, I feel more confident now that should some unthinkable mishap decide in its whimsy to pay another visit I might once more find the resources within to abide.

Esmeralda

Cal was a cop most of his adult life. He'd been in gunfights - seen the Elephant, as they say - and survived without a serious scratch from that dangerous career.

It was the other job that did him in, the one way back before he first pinned on a badge, the one that didn't put him deliberately in the harm's way cops choose as they preserve the peace and protect others from mayhem and violent death.

Cal died slowly from a hideous disease called "asbestosis," that took half a century to creep on clawed microscopic feet through his lungs and strangle him long after his exposure to asbestos working as a teenager with the nasty stuff building Navy ships.

I met him near the end of his police career, when he risked his retirement to help a news reporter root out corruption that involved some folks Cal knew. At one point, unbeknownst to me, he sat in his car out of sight while I interviewed a couple of subjects in the investigation. The interview was in a garage. The "subjects" were hostile. I bluffed my way back outside, which might have been a tad trickier had I known how concerned Cal was for my safety.

Bonded during this vocational relationship, which required absolute trust on both sides, we became friends and hunting/shooting buddies.

He told me about meeting, as a young Marine, Col. Charles Askins, who was helping set up a rifle team for a competition. Askins had a reputation as a "real hardass," Cal said, admitting to being nervous about meeting the living legend. When he did, he added, he found Askins to be gruff, but polite and respectful to the younger men. "He was a gentleman," Cal said.

It probably didn't hurt that the younger men knew well who their mentor was and treated him with the deference due a man of such stature.

Cal had pretty bad arthritis in his hands by the time I knew him, so he was limiting his shooting to rifles and skeet. Friends of his told me he'd once been a serious contender with handguns in competitive shooting. He was at the top of his game in 1983 when he shot against Rob Leatham and Ross Seyfried in the International Practical Shooting Confederation's World Shoot VI, which was held within tobacco-spitting distance of Cal's backyard.

I remember the event because our outdoor writer, a friend of Cal's who years later introduced us, did a story for the paper about a local gunsmith who fixed Seyfried's 1911 after its extractor broke during a match. Seyfried was the reigning IPSC champ, having won World Shoot V in his native Johannesburg, South Africa two years earlier. Leatham took the crown this time, winning his first of five IPSC world championships and launching an unparalleled career of shooting achievements.

The gun Cal used to put pressure on these giants was Esmeralda, a nickel plated Series 70 1911A1 .45 tricked out with nothing but an Aristocrat Rib. He'd done a little crude smithing on the piece, filing and buffing the ejection port a tad to reduce the chance of stovepipes, and adding a Colt rubber wraparound grip.

I found out he'd named it Esmeralda years after he sold it to me. Someone happened to mention it at the range once, and it seemed to embarrass him. I found out quite a bit later that Cal had borrowed the name from someone else, I believe it was Col. Jeff Cooper, who evidently had conferred the feminine moniker on his favorite 1911. I tried just now to confirm this in a Google search, but came up only with Exotic Grips by Esmeralda, which, if nothing else, definitely links the name to the right genre.

Anyway, Cal's 1911 will always be Ezzie to me. I've tricked her out a tad myself. Replaced the barrel with a Bar-Sto, replaced the Aristocrat Rib with Big Dot sights and replaced the Colt wraparound with a Crimson Trace equivalent.

I wish my childhood friend Mark could have had Ezzie handy the night he and his wife were murdered during a robbery at the business they owned together, years after I had last seen them. I don't know if he'd changed his thinking about guns by then. Maybe he no longer believed in their potential to save lives. Maybe his faith in others had become so strong he didn't feel the lethal danger some people carry with them, always. Maybe the laws in his community prohibited him from keeping a gun nearby for protection.

Maybe Mark had forgotten the saying people sometimes repeat when asked if they are willing to protect themselves even at the risk of violating a law, that it's better to be tried by twelve jurors than carried by six pallbearers.

I know one thing for sure. Had Mark been armed that night and willing to do whatever it took to save his life and that of his wife, and had he pulled out Ezzie or any gun capable of aiding him to that end, his would-be killers might just as well have been blackbirds flying overhead. Maybe Mark would have been tried for breaking some law, but you can believe this: no pallbearers would have been needed. Not then.

I haven't fired Ezzie in awhile, but she's always nearby when I'm at home or at the range. I'll hang onto her until I've matriculated to the next stage, where Cal and Mark and other passed friends have gathered.

Mathew Paust

About the Author

Mathew Paust was born and raised in a small town in Wisconsin. He is a former award-winning newspaper reporter who lives with his family in a wooded community in Virginia's Hampton Roads. Paust is also the author of *Executive Pink,* a satirical novel about presidential politics. Please visit his Web site at **www.mattpaust.com**.

CPSIA information can be obtained at www.ICGtesting.com
Printed in the USA
LVOW110942300512

283854LV00002B/76/P